THE FILLED PEN:
SELECTED NON-FICTIO

P.K. Page is best known as one of Canada's finest poets, but over the course of her career she has also written a number of essays – meditations – on her life and work, on the nature of art and the imagination, and on Canadian works of literature, painting, and film that have had special significance for her. As lovers of her poetry would hope and expect, these essays are beautiful, intelligent, moving, and delightfully quirky. *The Filled Pen* brings together the most important of these essays, including two previously unpublished: 'A Writer's Life' and 'Fairy Tales, Folk Tales: The Language of the Imagination.' Zailig Pollock, Page scholar and professor of English at Trent University, has edited and annotated this collection for admirers of Page's work, general readers, and academics alike.

The essays, which cover a period of approximately forty years, reflect Page's enduring concerns as a verbal and visual artist with the power of art and the imagination to transcend the barriers that limit our perceptions of the world and our sympathies with our fellow human beings. Page is more interested in posing questions than imposing answers; and fascinated as she is by a wide range of ideas, from ancient mysticism to modern neurophysiology, it is images, endlessly evocative and suggestive, that matter to her most. Her comments on A.M. Klein in 'A Sense of Angels,' one of the most moving and perceptive tributes by one poet to another, apply very much to the P.K. Page we see in *The Filled Pen*: 'For all his interest in the immediate world ... for all his acceptance of ideological and psychological theory, he seemed to reach beyond both to a larger reality.'

P.K. PAGE is a writer and painter living in Victoria B.C.

ZAILIG POLLOCK is a professor of English at Trent University.

The Filled Pen
Selected Non-fiction

P.K. Page
Edited by Zailig Pollock

UNIVERSITY OF TORONTO PRESS
Toronto Buffalo London

© P.K. Page 2007
© Editor's introduction and notes Zailig Pollock 2007
University of Toronto Press Incorporated
Toronto Buffalo London
Printed in Canada

ISBN-13: 978-0-8020-9108-6 (cloth)
ISBN-10: 0-8020-9108-3 (cloth)
ISBN-13: 978-0-8020-9399-8 (paper)
ISBN-10: 0-8020-9399-x (paper)

Printed on acid-free paper

Library and Archives Canada Cataloguing in Publication

Page, P. K. (Patricia Kathleen), 1916–
 The filled pen : selected non-fiction / edited by Zailig Pollock.

Includes index.
ISBN-13: 978-0-8020-9108-6 (bound)
ISBN-10: 0-8020-9108-3 (bound)
ISBN-13: 978-0-8020-9399-8 (pbk.)
ISBN-10: 0-8020-9399-x (pbk.)

I. Pollock, Zailig   II. Title.

PS8531.A34A16 2006   c818'.5409   c2006-903829-5

University of Toronto Press acknowledges the financial assistance to its publishing program of the Canada Council for the Arts and the Ontario Arts Council.

University of Toronto Press acknowledges the financial support for its publishing activities of the Government of Canada through the Book Publishing Industry Development Program (BPIDP).

To Connie

... the huge revolving world
the delicate nib releases.

from 'The Filled Pen'

Contents

ACKNOWLEDGMENTS ix
AUTHOR'S FOREWORD xi
EDITOR'S INTRODUCTION xiii

A Writer's Life 3
Safe at Home 23
Falling in Love with Poetry 29
Had I Not Been a Writer, What Would I Have Been? 32
Questions and Images 35
Traveller, Conjuror, Journeyman 43
Afterword to *A Flask of Sea Water* 48
Fairy Tales, Folk Tales: The Language of the Imagination 51
Foreword to *Hologram* 58
The Sense of Angels: Reflections on A.M. Klein 62
Notes on Re-reading George Johnston 69
Afterword to *The Innocent Traveller* 77
Afterword to *Emily's Quest* 82

Afterword to *Nights below Station Street* 87

Darkinbad the Brightdayler: The Work of Pat Martin Bates 92

The World of Maxwell Bates 98

Max and My Mother 101

Review of *The Company of Strangers* 109

TEXTUAL NOTES 113

INDEX 123

Acknowledgments

To Zailig Pollock, meticulous editor, who has left no comma unturned; to Théa Gray and Rosemary Sullivan, who insisted the book was worth publishing when I was at my most doubting; and to Farouk Mitha, who helped me assemble it in the first place, my loving appreciation.

Author's Foreword

I see myself primarily as a poet. This is perhaps because of all literary forms poetry is nearest to my heart. But in actual word count I have written much more prose. A youthful novel, short stories, travel writing – published and unpublished – plays, a libretto, children's books. Also I have spent many hours drawing and painting. My muse is restless. It seems to need new forms.

The prose in this book was written between 1969 and 2005. It was almost all solicited. The exceptions are 'Afterword to *A Flask of Sea Water*,' 'Fairy Tales, Folk Tales: The Language of the Imagination,' 'Notes on Re-reading George Johnston,' 'The World of Maxwell Bates,' and 'Max and My Mother.' I doubt that I would have written any of the other pieces had someone not asked me. Invitations seem to act like the 'given phrase' that so often starts a poem. But asked to address 'A Writer's Life,' I declined on the first invitation because I didn't think I could do it. I rarely think I can do it. Nor was I eager to write about myself. Imprinted by Eliot's 'objective correlative' in my twenties, his influence is with me still. Re-reading this manuscript, however, I realize that the self, like a child who has been put to bed before the party, cannot resist creeping downstairs.

P.K. Page
Victoria, BC, 2006

Editor's Introduction

In her essay on Lucy Maud Montgomery's *Emily's Quest*, P.K. Page, as if throwing down the gauntlet to prospective commentators on her own work, says, 'As a writer myself, I find irritating the belittling of the creative imagination implicit in the belief that all fiction is autobiographical.' She then continues, 'Yet in this case ...,'[1] and proceeds to explore, with all the respect due to a fellow artist, the interweaving of life and art in Montgomery's work. It is impossible to read the essays collected in *The Filled Pen* without becoming aware of a similar interweaving in Page's own writings. Although essays such as the ones on A.M. Klein and George Johnston can stand alone as essential reading for anyone interested in their subjects, all the essays, explicitly autobiographical or not, are 'endlessly mirroring mirrors'[2] in which Page sees herself: her own ambitions, struggles, and achievements. In this sense it is not, I think, a belittling of her creative imagination to view her essays as constituting a kind of autobiography – an autobiography of the imagination.

From this perspective, perhaps the most important of Page's essays is 'Questions and Images.' Her own comment on this and the closely related 'Traveller, Conjuror, Journeyman' is instructive: 'George Woodcock when he was editor of *Canadian Literature* solicited articles for an issue he was doing on autobiography. I told him I couldn't do what he asked but contributed these two pieces.'[3] In fact, Page did do what Woodcock asked, for these two pieces *are* autobiographies. But they are autobiographies of the imagination, the only kind of autobiography that Page is interested in writing. 'Questions and Images,' in particular, begins on a distinctly autobiographical note: 'The last ten years span three distinct places – and phases – in my life: Brazil, Mexico, Canada, in that order.'[4] But it quickly moves on to an account of the phases of Page's imaginative development, concluding with meditations on the nature of the imagination in general.

The title 'Questions and Images' used to strike me as awkward, as something of a non sequitur. Should it not be 'Questions and Answers' or 'Words and Images'? But as I have become more familiar with the shape and scope of Page's imagination, I have come to realize that the title is a perfect summary of her artistic ambitions and achievements.

Large questions have fascinated Page throughout her career, from the timeless insights of the 'perennial philosophy' to the tentative hypotheses of contemporary neuroscience. But she approaches these questions as an artist, not as a philosopher or a scholar or a critic. It is the evocative, mysterious questions themselves which interest her, not the provisional, incomplete answers that we often propose as a way of shutting down rather than opening up experience. What Page says of A.M. Klein is equally true of herself: 'for all his acceptance of ideological and psychological theory, he seemed to reach beyond both to a larger reality.'[5]

In Page's case, this larger reality manifests itself in images, whether visual or verbal (for her imagination is that of a painter as well as a poet), images which are often 'half-glimpsed, enigmatic,'[6] 'a sudden and momentary bouleversement.'[7] As she tells us in 'Fairy Tales, Folk Tales: The Language of the Imagination,' for her the language of the imagination is, in essence, a 'picture language – imaging, visualising – employing the right hemisphere ... [B]y working on ... the level of visualisation ... we can put ourselves into a relationship with the higher faculties of the mind.'[8]

To put this another way, although Page is a highly intelligent, cultivated commentator on life and art, there is something deeply unacademic about her writing. This is evident enough in her explicitly autobiographical essays, with their almost Proustian immediacy:

> When they carved in our much smaller house, I fell asleep to the sound of pounding mallets and ringing laughter – laughter of a kind that would sound somehow old-fashioned, innocent, today – and I wakened to crisp oak petals littering the floor, sharp and crunchy beneath my bare feet.[9]

> Drums from the *favelas* beat like one's own blood, accompanied by the deep bass viol of frogs in the lotus pond; volleys of rockets shattered the black night air, air wet as a sheet and rank with the smell of decaying jackos. Insistent, less obtrusive, the tiny fret of tropical vegetation, the sibilance of bamboos.[10]

But it is just as true of those essays that seem closest to traditional criticism, the ones in the second half of the collection dealing with the work of her fellow artists. One thing that surely sets these essays apart from the vast bulk of academic writing is the sheer beauty of their prose, which can be at the same time elegant, eloquent, funny, and precise – for example, her comments on the deceptive artlessness of George Johnston's poetry: 'The writing is as casual sounding as neighbours' talk. But poetry students take note: it is intricate as lace. Look for the rhymes and the half-rhymes – concealed as birds' nests.'[11] (And could this not be said of much of Page's own writing?) But what sets her essays apart even more definitively from typical academic writing is their essentially personal engagement with her subjects; or, perhaps it would be more accurate to say, their blending of the personal and (to use that word which is nowadays much derided) the universal.

Her essay on A.M. Klein, for example, begins with a poignant vignette, set against the exoticism of a Brazilian diplomatic soirée, describing her shock at hearing of the emotional collapse of her dear friend and colleague. At first, this section of the essay, beautifully written as it is, may strike us as irrelevant to the issue at hand, perhaps even self-indulgent. But upon repeated readings, Page's words, and the images they evoke, begin to resonate in 'half-glimpsed, enigmatic' ways with her celebration of Klein's 'familiar, sometimes exotic' art, which 'connect[s] and interlink[s] ... separate creeds, separate continents, separate spheres;'[12] and with her lament, as well, for the tragic isolation that was his fate:

> Imperial palms, their trunks floodlit, their feathered tops lost in the night sky, could have been free-standing Tuscan pillars ... Diplomatic uniforms, sashes, decorations; the black and white of tails; coloured silks and satins, diamonds, pearls; all mirrored in the water at our feet. Its mercurial silver-black received and submerged us topsy-turvy among the red tablecloths, the drowned pillars.[13]

Another example of Page's mingling of the personal and universal: her afterword to *Nights below Station Street* begins with a meditation on families in general, which then leads to a meditation on *her* family and finally to the mysterious interconnections between life and art:

> Families. A book about families ... All families. And timeless ... Completely different from my family, and completely different from yours – for what two families can possibly be the same? ...
>
> On the face of it, my parents were markedly unlike Rita and Joe, my younger sibling a temperamental opposite of Milly, and I doubt that anyone who knew me as a child would dream of comparing me with Adele ... But through Richards' portrayal of the Walshes, I know their family inside out. Even more remarkable, I could almost imagine they know mine. An absurd thought? How could fictional characters possibly know people in real life? It is beyond argument, I agree, but at some subliminal level, I suspect they might.[14]

A.M. Klein, George Johnston, Lucy Maud Montgomery, Topaz, Joe Walsh, Maxwell Bates, Pat Martin Bates, Page's mother, Rose ('in one way as invisible to me as I was to myself, in another she was the only one I saw')[15] – we come away from Page's accounts of these individuals, real and fictional, with vivid impressions of them all, but also with a vivid impression of Page herself, since in the end it is her imagination that has transformed this 'company of strangers'[16] and enabled us, her readers, to 'pass beyond personality, beyond character even, back to the primal matter of which we are all composed.'[17]

It is at Page's own insistence that her review of the film *The Company of Strangers* is the last essay in *The Filled Pen*, an insistence that never wavered through the volume's many stages of organization and reorganization. I will follow Page's example and end this introduction with a passage from her review of *The Company of Strangers*, which is one of the finest instances of her autobiography of the imagination, and which perfectly sums up my own experience of reading P.K. Page:

> If I think of the film in one way, I see it as a long green flowing continuity – a kind of banner with birds and music, splendid music. If I think of it in another, it is a series of perfect vignettes that recreate whole lives for us, that remind us of our friends, ourselves ...

So this is human existence, we say to ourselves as the credits roll. How wonderful it is. How valiant we are. How beautiful.[18]

Notes on This Edition

The essays collected in *The Filled Pen* constitute a relatively small proportion of P.K. Page's non-fictional prose over the last forty years. After extensive consultations with the author and with the University of Toronto Press, the decision was made to limit the selection to essays focusing on the arts; as well, we have decided not to include a number of essays on this theme, either because they seemed too slight for inclusion or because they duplicated material better presented elsewhere in the volume.

With two exceptions, all the essays in the collection have already appeared in print. The exceptions are 'A Writer's Life' and 'Fairy Tales, Folk Tales: The Language of the Imagination.' 'A Writer's Life' has previously appeared on the World Wide Web.

The textual notes to this edition list all previous publications. The texts have been collated against all published versions (including the Web version of 'A Writer's Life'), and the notes indicate all substantive variants. Minor variants in punctuation and layout have not been noted; nor have obvious typographical errors and errors in the transcription of passages that Page cites. (I have checked all of the latter with Page before correcting them against the texts being cited, to ensure that none of the changes were deliberate.) She is a persistent reviser – and improver – of her writing, and most of the essays in *The Filled Pen* show evidence of this. In most instances the revisions are relatively minor. The one major exception is the ending of 'Falling in Love with Poetry,' which has been substantially rewritten because of the close similarity of its original ending to the ending of 'Safe at Home.'

The primary function of the explanatory notes is to gloss obscure terms and references and to provide relevant information concerning Page's life and times. As with all such notes, it is difficult to know where to draw the line between providing readers with useful information and underestimating their cultural literacy. The perhaps controversial assumption has been made that for most readers of this volume, it is not necessary to identify major figures of Canadian literature or of world culture; so there are no notes identifying Al Purdy, for example, or Matisse. When biographical and bibliographical information is provided, it is kept to a minimum. I have deviated from this principle with one set of allusions, to Sufism and the perennial philosophy and to various figures, works, and concepts associated, at least in Page's view, with this tradition. Some examples are Idries Shah, Rumi, Titus Burckhardt, A.K. Coomaraswamy, Joseph Campbell, Carl Jung, Laurens van der Post, the Upanishads, *The Emerald Tablet*, *Primitive Mythology*, *Sacred Art in East and West*, 'tree on its head,' 'left brain/right brain,' and 'the thirty-six men.' These allusions, which are sometimes as 'concealed as birds' nests,' to quote Page's comment on George Johnston's rhyme schemes, seemed to me important enough to point out. Finally, Page is a wide-ranging but not particularly systematic reader, and even with her help, the sources of a few (not many) of her more recondite allusions and quotations remain unidentified.

This volume would not have been possible without the full and generous cooperation of P.K. Page. Théa Gray and Sandra Djwa supplied valuable advice and information at various stages of the project, and my research assistants Erin Reynolds and Robyn Letson provided much appreciated assistance with tracking down material, with annotation, and with proof-reading. My wife, Didi, was, as always, my most important sounding board and editor.

Zailig Pollock
Peterborough, Ontario, 2005

Notes

1. P. 86
2. 'Darkinbad the Brightdayler: The Work of Pat Martin Bates,' p. 94
3. 'Questions and Images,' p. 35n
4. P. 35
5. 'The Sense of Angels: Reflections on A.M. Klein,' pp. 64–5
6. 'Questions and Images,' p. 42
7. 'Questions and Images,' p. 41
8. P. 57
9. 'Max and My Mother,' pp. 103–4
10. 'Questions and Images,' p. 35

11 'Notes on Re-reading George Johnston,' p. 71
12 P. 68
13 P. 62
14 P. 87
15 'Max and My Mother,' p. 102
16 See 'Review of *The Company of Strangers*,' pp. 109–12
17 'Afterword to *Nights below Station Street*, p. 88
18 P. 111

THE FILLED PEN

A Writer's Life

Although I have been writing since I was a child, it is only within the last year or so that I have owned to the title of writer. It was the day the surveyor for the city directory came to the door. To her inquiry as to my profession, I said, 'Housewife.' 'Why didn't you say you were a writer?' my husband asked. 'Well, you know how doubtful I feel about my own work. It makes me uneasy claiming to be a writer.' He gave me a sharp look and said, 'She didn't ask you to say you were a good writer.'

At that moment I realised that, good or bad, I was, in fact, a writer, and that I had been for perhaps sixty-five years. Even so, I still have difficulties. The word 'writer' surely means one who writes. And I have spent most of my life not writing. Also, I am far from sure that I am the perpetrator of my own work. By that I don't mean I plagiarize – consciously, at least. But I do feel, as many writers do, that I am a vehicle, a channel for something that writes through me – badly sometimes, better at others. I cannot write if 'it' does not write me. I remember many years ago bumping into an old friend. 'What are you writing?' he asked. 'I'm not writing,' I replied. 'You mean you have given up poetry?' 'No, poetry has given up me.' 'Are you telling me that you are not the master?' he asked. 'Nor mistress,' I replied. That is still true for me of poetry. Less true of prose. I think I could guess the poets who would disagree with me.

'This hour long talk was twice solicited by the Writers' Development Trust. On the first invitation I refused. How could I possibly talk about my life as a writer? The second time I accepted. I delivered it to the AGM of The Canadian Writers' Union in Halifax in 1999'(PKP).

So much for the 'writer' side of the title. But 'life.' ... How do I tackle 'life'? The fact is, we live not one life but many, and this creature that answers to my name is not single, not simple, but multiple – a crowd. As well, the mind's eye is far from an accurate glass. When I recall my teenage years I see myself as solitary against the dun-coloured prairie where, from June to September, we pitched our tents and camped, swam in the muddy waters of the Elbow River and rode our horses into the foothills. My memory of the locale is accurate. But was my youthful figure so isolated? I think not. My parents encouraged children to be both seen and heard, and I recall no shortage of friends. Yet my essential self, the *self* concerned with rhythms and beats, was solitary and seldom shown until, summer ended, I returned to the city and the one friend who shared my interest in the arts.

We heard Debussy's *La Mer* in our heads as we cycled to school, pulled anguished faces at each other as her mother sang 'Trees' and spent hours poring over art books in the Calgary Public Library. There was not a wide selection but because we had no idea of what could be available, it never occurred to us that we were deprived. Epstein's break with realism excited us and – contrasted with the high romanticism of the Pre-Raphaelites – set up a curious counterpoint.

I remember the near-spell laid upon me by the reproduction of Dante Gabriel Rossetti's *How They Met Themselves* – a painting of a young couple in a wood, face to face with their clones; and of the shock of recognition when I read his 'Sudden Light' with its lines:

I have been here before
But when or how I cannot tell ...

Is there a built-in apparatus, which selects whatever one needs for one's own particular nourishment and development? Or is this as naïve a question as that of the child who wanted to know why the kitten's eyes were exactly behind those two little slits in its face?

Elbow River: running eastward from Elbow Lake towards Calgary, where it merges with the Bow River

'Trees': a popular middlebrow poem by American poet Joyce Kilmer. It was set to music by many composers.

Epstein: See note on 'Epstein's *Rima* ... Leicester Gallery' (p. 9).

Dante Gabriel Rossetti's *How They Met Themselves*: Rossetti was a British painter and poet and a founding member of the Pre-Raphaelite Brotherhood. *How They Met Themselves* is an interpretation of the legend of the Doppelgänger.

I am grateful to have grown up in an age when Grimm, Andersen, Perrault and the Arabian Nights were not considered too frightening for children. These tales must have laid a basis for my continuing acceptance of worlds other than this immediately tangible one – worlds where anything is possible – where one can defy gravity, become invisible, pass through brick walls. What appear as surrealist images in my work may stem from listening to such tales, and to my subsequent belief in the possible infiltration into our three-dimensional world, of our brothers, the gods. The content of folklore may well be metaphysics.

Talking to a young man at a party one night, when I said it was time I went home, he asked, 'How do you plan to go?' 'Oh, dematerialise and then teleport myself,' I replied. 'But *you* can't say that,' he exclaimed, 'you belong to a generation of rationalists.' So much for labels. I am reminded of a story in which an old lady was going from London to Edinburgh by train with her turtle. On a previous trip with her dog, she had had to buy a dog ticket. When she approached the ticket seller she asked if she would have to buy a ticket for her turtle. 'Oh, no, Mam,' he replied. 'Dogs is dogs and cats is dogs and rabbits is dogs. A squirrel in a cage is parrots. But turtles is insects and we don't charge for those.'

But to get back to adolescence when my conscious interest in poetry began. I see myself as a body of land struggling to emerge from an infinite surround of ocean. A sleeping land that moved about in its sleep.

> Heave me
> lift me
> out of this undreamed
> amorphous mound
> where who knows who
> lies sleeping
> my me I
> hidden
> unbidden still
> undead   unborn
> utterly unimaged even
>
> leaven me

Heave ... leaven me: from 'Waiting to Be Dreamed' (*HR* 2: 151–2); first published in *Canadian Forum* 50 (April–May 1970): 72

In these lines from a poem written many years later I was trying to recapture something of the feeling of that period. (Trying to recapture? Is that what I really mean? It is not the way poems are made – not mine, at any rate. How then, since we are on the subject, *are* poems made? With me they start, not so much from thoughts, as from a given line or rhythm, possibly a form. How they go on – or don't! – is another matter.)

I am sure that nobody, least of all myself, knew that while I played basketball and tennis, passed exams and wrote poems, that I was – as it were – underwater, asleep; or that my real business, the serious work I was intent upon – albeit subliminally – was that of awakening, surfacing, presenting my small sea-drenched island to the sun. For what purpose? Stonecrop? Vegetable marrow? A grove of palms? How could I foresee the use I would put it to?

This struggle to emerge continues still and will continue, I imagine, as long as I do. But whereas, now, the thought of emergence is relatively conscious, in adolescence it was undefined. The poetry, of course, was part of the struggle. The rhythms and beats, the inexpressible longings, the love poems – oh to whom? – were all part of the 'upward anguish'; while the good serve at tennis, when I achieved it, or the high mark in algebra, occurred in the world of my daylight self.

Looking back at that period of my life from this vantage point, I would say that the right hemisphere of my brain – the dreaming, intuitive, creative hemisphere – was battling with a system of education intent upon developing the rational, logical, lineal left.

Calgary, in the years I grew up, was a sportsman's town. Many of my parents' friends were ranchers who came to town on horseback. One friend of my mother's, impeccably habited, and mounted side-saddle, would arrive for afternoon tea with a gift of a live chicken struggling in a burlap bag. It wasn't until many years later in Mexico, that I received a similar gift – this time presented by the mother of a girl who worked for

---

stonecrop: 'a herb with bright yellow flowers and small cylindrical fleshy sessile leaves, growing in masses on rocks, old walls, etc.' (*OED*)
vegetable marrow: (chiefly Brit.) 'any of various kinds of squash or gourd ... eaten as a vegetable' (*OED*)
upward anguish: a reference to *The Upward Anguish*, an autobiography by British author Humbert Wolfe
right hemisphere ... lineal left: See note on 'Robert Ornstein' (p. 56).

us, and whom we had saved from a ruptured appendix. The mother had travelled countless miles by crowded bus, with her laying hen and her *setesima*. A *setesima* is a seven-month baby. The fact that a premature child can survive in primitive conditions is so extraordinary that its very presence confers good luck on all who encounter it. I was ill in bed at the time, and before I knew what had happened, I found the broody hen, the baby and I were all snuggled down between the sheets.

But to go back. The Calgary of the late twenties, early thirties, seemed hardly conducive to fostering artists, yet it produced the painter, Maxwell Bates. His parents and mine were friends and spent many winter evenings wood carving, taking their designs from 'art nouveau' magazines. Within my home circle, as with the prairie landscape, shapes and their relation to space were an unspoken part of my life. As I wrote much later, thinking of the prairie:

> One's self the centre of a boundless circle
> So balanced in its horizontal plane
> And sensitively tuned that one's least move
> Could fractionally tip it east, north, south.
> Westward, in undulations of beige turf
> The fugal foothills changed their rhythms, rose
> To break in fire and snow. My Hindu Kush.

One was indeed smacked by infinity's vast hand.

Adolescence, that great releaser of hormones, must also take responsibility for masses of bad poems. Mine were mainly about suffering. As I think of it now, I had little to suffer about except, I suppose, the turbulence that goes with one's teens. Unlike many of my writing friends, I had no reason to complain about my parents. They both came from families that had produced artists and writers and they, themselves, were artists *manqués*. They encouraged me, urged me to send poems to whatever magazines might print them. When I actually had a poem accepted, I

Maxwell Bates: See 'The World of Maxwell Bates' (pp. 98–100) and 'Max and My Mother' (pp. 101–8).
One's self ... Hindu Kush: from 'The First Part' (*HR* 1: 216–19); first published in *The West Coast Review* (February 1979): 5–6. The version printed here differs slightly from other published and unpublished versions.

took refuge in the initials P.K. for fear my school friends would recognise me. It has been suggested that I chose initials to hide my gender. Not true. At that point I was far too unobservant and unworldly to have taken in the fact that most writers were men. But I did know that writing poetry simply wasn't done! Eating with your knife was preferable.

At seventeen, my schooling behind me, I had no intention of going on to university. I was not a student. Curiously, almost no literature had fired my imagination, certainly no Canadian literature. But that is not entirely the case. Did I not give a speech in Grade 9 about Ernest Thompson Seton's animal stories? And do I not vaguely remember poems by Pauline Johnson, Marjorie Pickthall and Drummond? All of them in subject matter no less foreign to me than Keats' 'Ode to a Nightingale' and nowhere near as full of wonder as those 'magic casements opening on the foam' or Coleridge's 'caverns measureless to man.' It was not that I had read nothing – I had read omnivorously – Gene Stratton-Porter, Hugh Walpole, Charles Morgan, endless historical romances, but I had no idea of the flavour of contemporary writing until I found myself in England with a membership in Boots' remarkable library system. There I stumbled, blind, upon Virginia Woolf. She was my first great literary discovery and I was totally unprepared for her. I opened *The Waves* and read without drawing breath:

> I see a ring, said Bernard, hanging above me. It quivers and hangs in a loop of light.
> I see a slab of pale yellow, said Susan, spreading away until it meets a purple stripe.

---

the initials P.K.: Page's earliest published poems, 'Current Events' and 'On Being Ill,' appeared in *The Ammonite*, the newspaper of St Hilda's School for Girls in Calgary, Alberta: 5 (1932): 30, and 6 (1933): 16, respectively. The byline for these poems is 'P. Page.' 'P.K. Page' first appears as the byline for her next published poem, 'The Moth,' in the London *Observer*, 2 December 1934, 35.

'magic casements opening on the foam': from John Keats' 'Ode to a Nightingale'

'caverns measureless to man': from Samuel Taylor Coleridge's 'Kubla Khan'

Gene Stratton-Porter: an American author and naturalist who wrote principally about the American Midwest; Hugh Walpole: a British novelist best known for his family saga *The Herries Chronicle*; Charles Morgan: a British dramatic critic and novelist

Boots' remarkable library system: Boots, a British pharmacy chain, provided 'Booklovers' Libraries' from which members could borrow.

I hear a sound, said Rhoda, cheep, chirp; cheep chirp; going up and down.

I see a globe, said Neville, hanging down in a drop against the enormous flanks of some hill.

I see a crimson tassle, said Jinny, twisted with gold threads.

I hear something stamping, said Louis. A great beast's foot is chained. It stamps, and stamps, and stamps.

This marvellously rhythmic prose turned my heart to water. I burst into tears, and fell in love with words.

I also discovered Edith Sitwell:

Jane, Jane,
Tall as a crane,
The morning light creaks down again.

Creaks! It was as if I had found a friend. I am sure we all are born synaesthetic but we learn to keep quiet about it. Adults tell us it is not possible. But here was an adult, a published adult, who clearly knew of it, too. I had, of course, not yet read Rimbaud. Nor had I discovered Eliot or Auden or Yeats or Pound. Clearly, I was retarded. Compared with what travelling young people see and hear today when they go abroad, I was an ignoramus. But during that seminal twelve months I actually saw Epstein's *Rima* in Hyde Park and his *Ecce Homo* on exhibition in the Leicester Gallery.

I was a romantic, of course. How could I have been anything else? If the prairies – aided by Zane Grey's novels – had not made me one, Russian ballet would have. And my writing style, if style it was, was hopelessly romantic. Starting in grade school I wrote narrative poems. My earliest, about Napoleon, was in fact, an epic. It began:

Edith Sitwell: Jane ... down again: British poet. The quotation is from 'Aubade.'
Rimbaud: The reference is to 'Voyelles,' the synaesthetic sonnet by French poet Arthur Rimbaud, beginning 'A noir, E blanc, I rouge, U vert, O bleu: voyelles.'
Epstein's *Rima* ... Leicester Gallery: Sir Jacob Epstein was an American-born British sculptor. His statue in Hyde Park of Rima, a beautiful young woman of the forests in *Green Mansions* by W.H. Hudson, caused great controversy. His *Ecce Homo* was one of a series of statues on religious themes. Page describes the effect this statue had on her in her poem 'Ecce Homo,' first published in *Contemporary Verse* 1, 1 (September 1941): 5–6 (*HR* 1: 17–18).

> Napoleon, as a boy, we're told
> Was ever noble, ever bold.
> And this short poem will show to you
> What a young boy can really do.

I tried my hand at free verse. I acquired a book on prosody and wrote triolets, sonnets, villanelles – about love, requited and un.

When I returned to Canada a year later I had had one poem published in the London *Observer*, had lost my heart to Russian Ballet, George Bernard Shaw and modern art. I was more eyes than brains; a dreamer rather than a planner, and my future stretched before me – blank.

My family had moved from Alberta to New Brunswick. There I joined them, astonished to find that this too was Canada. New Brunswick gave me the excitement of a creative community. I met poets, potters, painters, theatre people – Kay Smith, the Deichmanns, Miller Brittain, Jack Humphrey. I wrote masses of bad verse, and a youthful novel, *The Sun and the Moon*. It was about a girl who turned into a tree. Of *course* one can become a tree. Daphne did; and Baucis and Philemon and all Phaeton's grieving sisters. The MS went the usual rounds of publishers and ended up at Macmillan in Toronto. They offered to publish it as soon as the paper shortage ended. I was ecstatic! I wrote plays for children's theatre, and even acted myself, having come back from England stage-struck and unfocussed. Did I want to write or act?

I immersed myself in Ibsen. *Peer Gynt* and *An Enemy of the People* represented the poles of my interests – the imaginative/symbolic, on the one hand, and social criticism on the other – interests which, when I emerged from a protective family into the more sophisticated and contemporary

---

prosody ... villanelles: Page's early verse manuscripts in the Page fonds in Library and Archives Canada, especially the first two, dating from her late teens and early twenties (box 1, files 1 and 2), contain many examples of poems in these forms. The first of these also contains extensive notes on prosody.

one poem ... *Observer*: 'The Moth'; see note on 'the initials P.K.' above.

Kay Smith ... Jack Humphrey: Kay Smith, poet; Kjeld and Erica Deichmann, potters; Miller Brittain and Jack Humphrey, painters

The Sun and the Moon: published in 1944 by Macmillan under the pseudonym Judith Cape; republished in 1973 by Anansi Press in *The Sun and the Moon and Other Fictions*, edited by Margaret Atwood, under Page's own name

plays for children's theatre: Scripts for some of these plays can be found in box 4 of the Page fonds in Library and Archives Canada.

world of Montreal, polarized around Jung and Marx. I had neither a Jungian analysis nor did I become a Marxist, but the great continents of myth and seas of dream, uncovered and explored by Jung, and the Marxist vision of a world in which all men and women are privileged, could not help but stir me. Perhaps Utopia *was* possible – personally and communally – the one through individuation, the other through politics.

I arrived in Montreal from the Maritimes early in World War II. The whole idea of going off alone to a strange city was totally foreign to my friends. But I knew there was another world. I had already tasted it.

I rented a room in a boarding house and wrote every morning from 9 to 12 just like a real writer – living on a minute allowance given me by my father. But it was not long before I realised that if independence was what I wanted, I had better not accept financial help from home. So, ill equipped as I was, I found a job in an office that handled blue prints and specifications for small arms.

This was wartime – a time of rationing, and grief. My poems about offices were written at this period – poems about stenographers and typists. It was not my first job – I had worked in a department store in Saint John, New Brunswick and already had an idea of how abused unorganised workers could be. Much of my poetry reflected these ideas – poems of social criticism, often expressed in the images of dream. I suppose it was as near as I ever came to polemics.

A few months after I arrived in Montreal the long arm of chance introduced me to the young English poet, Patrick Anderson. He invited me to attend a meeting of a recently formed literary group – the Preview group – which was planning to produce a small magazine – although 'This is not a magazine' ran the first editorial. And indeed, it was not; it was a handful of mimeographed pages held together by a staple. You should remember, you who have grown up in an age with the Canada Council and a proliferation of little magazines, that in the early forties, throughout the entire country, only two magazines regularly published poetry,

---

poems about stenographers and typists: 'The Stenographers' was first published in the *Canadian Forum* 22, 260 (September 1942): 177 (HR 1: 102–3); 'Typists' in *Preview*, February 1943, (2–3) (HR 1: 103). Other poems on similar themes from this period are 'Offices,' *Preview* 16 (October 1943): 8 (HR 1: 100), and 'Shipbuilding Office,' *Preview* 15 (August 1943): 4 (HR 1: 104).
poems of social criticism ... images of dream: for example, 'Prediction without Crystal,' *First Statement* 1 (October 1942): 6–7 (HR 1: 101).

the poets themselves were just emerging from their closets, and World War II was raging in Europe. Naturally there was no money for anything unrelated to the war effort.

The first Preview meeting I attended was at F.R. Scott's house. Present were Scott, Anderson, Bruce Ruddick, Neufville Shaw, and Margaret Day, plus a few partners and friends – all strangers to me but for Anderson, briefly met. I had been asked to bring some poems with me and they were passed around and read in solemnity and silence. Never had any poetry seemed as bad in my eyes as mine at that moment. Finally Scott said, 'Bones! My God, here's a girl who writes about bones. You can't write about bones anymore.' After such silence, it seemed the kindest remark I had ever heard. Nothing further was said about my work, so I presumed there would be no return engagement. But as the meeting broke up, Anderson said, 'Miss Page' – a formal fellow was Patrick – 'our next meeting will be held on ...' and he gave me a date and place. And so I became a member of the Preview group.

It was a heady time for me and, set on fire by Patrick's imagery, coupled with the whole experience of living in a large bi–lingual city and working in wartime offices, I could barely keep myself in enough paper to get everything down – poetry and prose. Nor could I take in the rush of ideas I was exposed to.

Having come from a military family where politics were never discussed, I now found myself in the thick of discussions on both local and international politics. With Anderson a Communist and Scott a socialist, I had an early lesson in the differences between the two.

Meanwhile I was reading – Tolstoy, Dostoevsky, Gogol, to say nothing of Eliot, Yeats and Pound. The second phase of my education had begun. I made just enough money to keep myself modestly, and I became friends with a number of writers and painters – A.J.M. Smith, A.M. Klein, Jori Smith, Goodridge Roberts – all of whom in their various ways, contributed to quickening my eye and my ear.

Finally Scott said ... bones anymore: The poem was 'Desiring Only' (e-mail from P.K. Page, 25 October 2005). Along with 'No Flowers,' it was the first poem of Page's to appear in *Preview*, in the April 1942 issue (HR 1: 20). In *Like One That Dreamed: A Portrait of A.M. Klein* (McGraw-Hill Ryerson, 1982), 51, Usher Caplan reports a similar anecdote of Scott and A.J.M. Smith objecting to a sonnet by A.M. Klein because it had the word 'soul' in it. However, in Klein's case, the sonnet was ultimately not accepted by them for publication.
Jori Smith: painter and lifelong friend of Page
Goodridge Roberts: painter

There was never, I think, an issue of *Preview* without something of mine in it. As well as publishing regularly in *Preview* and *Contemporary Verse*, occasionally in John Sutherland's *New Statement* and, during Earle Birney's editorship, *The Canadian Poetry Magazine*, I had work accepted also by *Poetry: A Magazine of Verse*, in Chicago. Caught up in this new world, I had completely forgotten that *The Sun and the Moon* was on a back burner at Macmillan's until the day I received a telegram saying they were all set to publish. Only too eager to see the book in print when I had written it, I now had serious misgivings. In doubt as to what to do, I asked a friend. He said that as I had written it in good faith I should go ahead, using a pseudonym if that made me feel better. And so I did. *The Sun and the Moon* by Judith Cape came out in 1944 to little acclaim. But like all events, it had a ripple effect: the first being the book's republication in 1973 when I claimed it as my own; the second when it was dramatised by Peter Haworth and produced by Don Mowatt on CBC radio.

My first book of poems, *As Ten as Twenty*, was published in 1946 by The Ryerson Press. At that time Ryerson was almost our only publisher interested in poetry. Looking back I find it astonishing that they accepted my slim 43-page manuscript consisting of random poems. Sequences of poems – a commonplace today – were uncommon then. It may be that the Canada Council, by asking grant applicants for project outlines, began the trend.

At about this time, I got a job with the National Film Board as a writer for filmstrips. I had no great dreams of writing for film, although I think I had a natural instinct for letting the visuals do the talking. The wide variety of subjects I had to tackle filled in many gaps in my education and I gained a certain confidence that I could – after a fashion – write for a living. I wrote the script and commentary for an animated film, sponsored by the Department of Health. It was about teeth and was entitled, *Teeth Are to Keep*. It won an award at Cannes. My finest hour!

In 1954, my second book of poems, *The Metal and the Flower*, appeared. It was the 7th in the Indian File series begun by Jack McClelland – a series-title that would be unacceptable today! It was well received wherever it was that books *were* received in those days – the *Canadian Forum*, perhaps

---

Peter Haworth: Canadian actor and CBC broadcaster and frequent contributor to the *Ideas* series

Don Mowatt: producer of radio features and drama at the CBC and frequent contributor to the *Ideas* series

– and it won a Governor-General's Award. We were in Australia when the award was announced and in the circles where I moved, which were mainly diplomatic, few people knew I wrote. One acquaintance, after reading the book, looked at me in astonishment and said, 'I shall never again know what you are thinking.' She must have been more of a fiction writer than I, because it had never occurred to me that I knew *her* thoughts. The remark has made me wonder if perhaps that is the reason I have never felt comfortable with fiction.

During our years in Australia I wrote poetry – in the main placeless, as my poetry is apt to be – and intermittent notes about a country that fascinated and appalled me. I read Australian literature with curiosity but without admiration. Their novels informed, but failed to engage me; their poetry was still Georgian. I must remind you that this was in the fifties and things have changed radically since then. Pre-computer, pre-TV, the world did not have the simultaneity it has today and time lags were very apparent.

I was intrigued by aboriginal bark drawings – as I still am. Because they arise out of ceremonial and belief, rather than neurosis or loss, they seem closer in spirit to early European religious paintings than to the work of contemporary artists. For some mysterious reason, they are personal to me – all that stipple and cross-hatching.

I was fascinated by the southern hemisphere: the Southern Cross in the night sky, kangaroos pogo-sticking across the outback; koala bears snoring in the eucalypts; and actually in our garden, multicoloured parrots, wrens as blue as Brazilian blue butterflies, and a bird with the scream of a madwoman. I have always been a nature buff. Small wonder I was enthralled.

If Australia fascinated me, Brazil, where we went next, fascinated me still more. Here the butterflies were as blue as Australian blue wrens! It was also my first immersion in the baroque – its architecture, its vegetation, its people. I fell in love with it totally. But it took away my tongue. I had no matching vocabulary. It was painful for me to be unable to write, but by some alchemy the pen that had written, began to draw. *It* drew everything *I* saw. Drew in a way I would be unable to draw today, and

---

aboriginal bark drawings: See 'Bark Drawing,' first published in the *Tamarack Review* 44 (Spring 1967): 7–8 (HR 2: 117–18).

eased the pain of writer's block – or what I thought of as writer's block. Actually, I *was* writing – almost daily – but because it was not poetry, it didn't feel like writing. What I produced – very often with a marmoset on my shoulder examining my hair for nits – were voluminous notes to be published later by Lester & Orpen Dennys as *Brazilian Journal*.

During our time in Brazil, and in Mexico which followed, drawing and painting obsessed me. In Mexico I had the good luck to meet the surrealist painter, Leonora Carrington, who taught me how to use egg tempera. I taught myself to lay gold leaf. Not easy! The least breath while handling the delicate foil will send it flying and what you see in your hand if you are quick enough to catch it looks like nothing more than a crushed clothes moth. *Or Volador* the Spanish call it – flying gold. It is well named. I kept a journal once again, parts of which have appeared in magazines, and it has been my intention to consolidate it and make a book of it, but it *does* feel like the past, and the older I grow the more I want to live in the present.

In 1967, in Canada once again, McClelland & Stewart published a book of new and selected poems – *Cry Ararat!* – a poor title for a non-biblical age, and frequently referred to – I might add! – as *Cry A Rat.* Beautifully designed by Stan Bevington, it includes the first of my black-and-white drawings to appear in book form. It was my re-emergence after years abroad.

In response to proddings from George Woodcock, I wrote two essays in which I attempted to explain my reactions to northern North America after roughly ten years in a Latin culture. In one I say, 'The culture shock of homecoming after many years abroad is even greater, I think, than the

---

Brazilian Journal: published in 1987
Leonora Carrington: British-born Mexican surrealist painter and writer
egg tempera: 'a method of painting, in which the colours are mixed with some glutinous substance soluble in water, as yolk of egg mixed with water, etc., executed usually upon a ground of chalk or plaster mixed with gum' (*OED*)
Stan Bevington: founder of Coach House Press, a small Toronto publishing company known for publishing the early works of authors such as Margaret Atwood and Michael Ondaatje
George Woodcock: Canadian poet, essayist, critic, and biographer; founded the journal *Canadian Literature* in 1959
two essays: 'Questions and Images' (pp. 35–42) and 'Traveller, Conjuror, Journeyman' (pp. 43–7)

culture shock of entering a new country. One returns different, to a different place, misled by the belief that neither has changed.'

An obvious and radical change was in the poetry scene. Ryerson, McClelland & Stewart, and Oxford were publishing more poetry; a number of small publishing houses had sprung up; there were more poets; and poetry readings had begun – an unheard of activity! This astonishing change was undoubtedly thanks to the CBC, which provided a stage for Canadian writers, and to the Canada Council, which had not existed when we left Canada in the early fifties.

I soon realised that if I were to be part of this scene, I would have to give readings. My first – at the invitation of Al Purdy when he was Writer-in-Residence at Simon Fraser – was to Sandra Djwa's English class. I was terrified in advance, but as with many things in my life, once I had taken the plunge, not only was I unafraid – I actually enjoyed it. I did a small tour in BC with Margaret Atwood – a young star; a winter Maritime tour that took me to PEI by a ferry that doubled as icebreaker; and a tour of England with Earle Birney and Michael Ondaatje. I loved the chance to meet fellow-poets, talk to students, and make new friends. On the debit side, I was disappointed that the academe I had so greatly respected – partly, I suppose, because I had not been to university – was often inflexible and doctrinaire.

During this period Margaret Atwood collected my youthful novel, together with some of my early short fiction and published *The Sun and the Moon and Other Fictions,* the first of Anansi's *Found Books.* The following year, believing rightly, that if my work were in hard cover only, I would never be put on a university curriculum, she edited a paperback, *Poems Selected and New.* The whole philosophy of hard versus soft covers, an interesting subject, has changed greatly in my lifetime but this is not the place to go into it.

In the seventies, I edited a book of short poems, *To Say the Least: Canadian Poets from A-Z* which, if read consecutively from beginning to end, is a poem in itself. What inspired me was listening to my mother as an old lady reciting reams of Shakespeare, Wordsworth and Tennyson. It gave her great pleasure. I thought how deprived we are today by not having

---

Sandra Djwa: literary scholar and critic and biographer of Page
The Sun and the Moon and Other Fictions: published in 1973
Poems Selected and New: Anansi Press, 1974
To Say the Least: Canadian Poets from A-Z: Press Porcepic, 1979

been made to learn poetry by heart. And how, with our shortened attention spans, we could probably memorise only poems as brief as F.R. Scott's

> Is
> is not
> the end of Was
> or start of Will Be
> Is
> is
> Is.

Or Eldon Grier's

> I am almost asleep
> with your poems on my chest,
>
> Apollinaire
>
> I am almost asleep
> but I feel a transfusion of fine little letters
> dripping slantwise into my side.

Or my poem, 'Truce':

> My enemy in a purple hat
> looks suddenly like a plum
> and I am dumb with wonder at the thought
> of feuding with a fruit.

Because I was devoting more time to it, the pace of my literary life was quickening. I taught for summers at Jerry Lampert's Writers' Workshop

---

Eldon Grier: Canadian artist and poet who studied under Diego Rivera in Mexico
'Truce': first published in *Poems Selected and New*, 121 (HR 2: 81)
Jerry Lampert's Writers' Workshop in Toronto: Gerald Lampert was an arts administrator who took a special interest in the work of young writers.

in Toronto – terrified once again. What did I know that could possibly be useful to anyone?

I wrote a long short story, 'Unless the Eye Catch Fire' based on a dream. Or was it? Some of it was. It is a story about an ordinary woman who suddenly sees her world transformed. At the same time, barely noticeably at first, the temperature is increasing. The story appeared as a prose centrepiece to a book of poems, *Evening Dance of the Grey Flies,* published in the fall of 1981. Since then it has been performed as a one-woman show by Joy Coghill. *Evening Dance ...* arrived in my hands from Oxford the day our local paper ran a story with a New York Times by-line, that began, 'Strong new evidence that carbon dioxide pollution is causing a potentially dangerous warming of the earth's climate ...' etc. etc. My short story was written in the late 70's, before any talk of global warming had reached the press. I am not trying to suggest that I have prophetic powers. I haven't. But it does make me ask myself something about dreams. What are they? Where do they originate? Surely they are not merely the garbage pails of our lives, as some psychologists would suggest. I suspect that all of us here know the qualitative differences between dreams. Some are patently rubbish. But the others ...? How can one help but wonder. Are they perhaps an escape hatch to a higher realm?

> Those people in a circle on the sand
> are dark against its gold
> turn like a wheel
> revolving in a horizontal plane
> whose axis – do I dream it? –
> vertical
> invisible
> immeasurably tall
> rotates a starry spool.

So begins a poem based entirely on dream.

Evening Dance of the Grey Flies: Oxford University Press
Joy Coghill: Canadian actor, director, and writer
Those people ... spool: from 'Another Space,' first published in *Poetry* (Chicago) 114 (August 1969): 299–300 (HR 2: 170–1)

The eighties diversified me. Murray Adaskin, commissioned by the Victoria Symphony Orchestra to compose a musical score for children based on *The Musicians of Bremen*, asked me to write the text. The story, as I read it, is about team spirit and the triumph of art. The beauty of folk/fairy tales is that – like poems, or like *anything*, come right down to it – what you see in them is what is in them for you. I try to tell students this – and so run counter to the prevailing analytical methods of teaching.

That year I also put together a selected poems, *The Glass Air*. It had as its cover an egg-tempera painting by me and contained drawings and two essays. In 1991, re-printed as *The Glass Air: Poems Selected and New*, it included a convocation address, given at Simon Fraser, and written in verse. I had watched ruthless developers mindlessly destroying our rain forest, I had heard a voice saying 'It doesn't matter what you do as long as you serve your planet,' and I was split about the role of the artist. In such an extreme situation, should the artist become an activist or should he/she believe absolutely in the redemptive power of art? Better still, embrace both? Towards the end of my address I say:

> But to get back to art, for there my heart is,
> there – beyond materiality,
> beyond the buy-and-sell, beyond the want
> embedded in us, and beyond desire –
> resides the magic greed has cancelled out.
> If we'll but give it time, a work of art
> 'can rap and knock and enter in our souls'
> and re-align us – all our molecules –
> and make us whole again. A work of art,
> could, 'had we but world enough and time,'
> portray for us – all Paradise apart –
> 'the face we had before the world was made ...'

Murray Adaskin: Canadian composer and violinist
The Musicians of Bremen: published as *The Travelling Musicians* (Kids Can Press, 1991)
The Glass Air ... egg-tempera painting: Oxford University Press, 1985; second edition, 1991. The cover reproduces a detail of *The Garden* (1961).
convocation address: 'Address at Simon Fraser University' was delivered at the 1990 convocation. It was first published in the *Canadian Forum* 70, 802 (September 1991): 20–1 (HR 2: 99–104).

Still in the 80's, encouraged by George Woodcock and Michael Ondaatje, I began work on a period piece based on the notes I made in Brazil. Perhaps this is the moment to say that more than thirty years earlier I had married Arthur Irwin – a man with a formidable reputation as an editor. I had seen strong men blench beneath his editorial gaze and had, as a result, rarely asked his advice about my work. By 1987 I must have felt brave, for I enlisted his help with *Brazilian Journal*. It was one of the exceptionally happy periods of our life. He worked on the MS, section by section, and passed his comments on to me. I acted upon them or not – almost invariably the former – and was astonished to discover that a good editor is one who actually makes you more yourself.

At about that time I was asked by Don Mowatt to write a poem for radio about Sibelius. I was far from sure I could write to order in this way. But I borrowed or bought all Sibelius' recorded music, read what little the library could provide about his life, and was drawn into reading the *Kalavela* – creation myth and Finnish national epic – parts of which he had used as texts for his songs. Its form and scope were a revelation to me. I flooded the house with his music, and finally, not without surprise, wrote a half hour piece for two voices entitled 'I – Sphinx.' It was performed on CBC radio with a young Finnish composer in the role of Sibelius with me as narrator.

We live in Victoria, my husband and I, but Arthur's roots are in Ontario, and so for many summers we travelled east to cottage country where fourteen grandchildren learned to swim and handle boats and get to know the family face. One summer I began making up a fairy story about a poor boy who lived in a land-locked kingdom. Day after day the story grew. It was criticised by the sophisticated members of my juvenile audience, who *knew* that love at first sight is impossible, and animals don't talk. Despite their derision, I finished what was finally published as *A Flask of Sea Water*. A sequel, *The Goat That Flew*, followed. Having grown up on fairy tales, it was not unnatural for me to write

---

Kalavela: based on folk poems compiled and edited by Elias Lönnrot in 1835
'I – Sphinx': performed on 'Aircraft' on the CBC in March 1989; first published in *Exile* 14 (Summer 1989): 53–64 (HR 2: 135–44)
A Flask of Sea Water: Oxford University Press, 1989
The Goat That Flew: Victoria: Beach Holme Publishers, 1994

them. I agree with Joseph Campbell that they are 'the picture language of the soul.'

In the 1990's I encountered the *glosa,* a form used by the Court poets in mediaeval Spain. Fourteen *glosas* later I published *Hologram*. Since then Stan Dragland has edited my collected poems – *The Hidden Room*; and Francesca Valente translated a selection of my work into Italian in a book entitled, *Compass Rose.*

I could go on, but the speech I had thought would be a creed, a philosophy, or an aesthetic has turned into a laundry list. Let me try to save it.

I have never belonged to a school. I have been in love with, but not wedded to, form. I believe with Graves that the theme chooses the poet; with Salvador Dali that to gaze is to think; and with Goethe that 'The beautiful is a manifestation of secret laws of Nature, which, but for this appearance, had been forever concealed from us.'

I suspect that metre is a brain-altering drug – one we ignore at our peril. Just consider what we know, but take for granted: that iambic is the lub-dub of the heart, and iambic pentameter that lub-dub repeated five times – roughly the number of heartbeats to a breath. It is difficult for me to believe this is accidental.

I believe art has two functions: a lower and a higher. The lower is invaluable. It shows us ourselves – Picasso's *Guernica*, for example. The

---

Joseph Campbell ... picture language of the soul': from *The Flight of the Wild Gander: Explorations in the Mythological Dimension* (Viking Press, 1969), 37. For Joseph Campbell, see note to 'Joseph Campbell ... Jungian' (p. 56).
glosa: see 'Forward to *Hologram*' (pp. 58–61)
Hologram: Brick Books, 1994
Stan Dragland: Canadian editor and publisher; founded *Brick: A Journal of Reviews* and Brick Books, a poetry publishing house
The Hidden Room: Porcupine's Quill, 1997
Francesca Valente: Italian translator and editor, involved in the direction of the Italian Cultural Institute in Canada and the United States
Compass Rose: *Rosa dei vente* (Longo Editore, 1998)
Graves ... the poet: Robert Graves, British poet, novelist and critic; 'In poetry ... the theme is always new and chooses the poet' ('Lecture One, 1964,' in *Poetic Craft and Principle: Lectures and Talks by Robert Graves* [Cassell, 1967]), 7
Goethe ... concealed from us.': This quotation from Goethe's *Maxims and Reflections* (number 183) has achieved currency in the English-speaking world by being quoted in Emerson's esssay 'Beauty.' Page cites Emerson's translation here and in 'Falling in Love with Poetry' (p. 31).

higher – more valuable still, in my view – gives us glimpses of another order. If I may quote from my poem, 'Poor Bird':

> in the glass of a wave a painted fish
> like a work of art across his sight
> reminds him of something he doesn't know
> that he has been seeking his whole long life –

So, where do I go from here? I have no idea. The journey is without maps. But when I glance back, as I have tonight, to where I have been, I know that the life of the artist is one of the most privileged of all lives.

I would have chosen no other way.

(1999)

'Poor Bird': a *glosa*, first published in *Prairie Schooner* 67 (Winter 1993): 24–5 (HR 2: 195–6)

Safe at Home

Home. A mutable word as I now know. But when I was a child it meant only one thing: being with my parents. In a bungalow in Calgary during bitter winters, logs burning in the hearth. Under canvas in a bell tent on the prairie, where I tethered my horse to a stake, crocuses already pushing up through late snow. In a bare Winnipeg military barracks that smelled of shoe polish and *Brasso*. Or exploring the magical drawers of cabinets that housed collections of birds' eggs too fragile to touch (all neatly catalogued and arranged by unknown uncles) and shells from foreign seas: cream or pink or leopard-spotted, cowries, cone shells, and ears of mother-of-pearl. *Indian Ocean*, read one label and *S. Shore of Africa* another. This was in my grandparents' house – lodestone and lodestar, both.

No matter the place, if my parents were there, it was home. Home meant love, security, safety; laughter too, and talk.

In Calgary, when I was a pre-kindergarten only child before my brother was born, my mother created whole communities, which we cut out together, made three-dimensional. She should have been a maker of children's games. She *was* a maker of children's games. But she made them for me alone. Villages with church, school, shops, thatched houses, arrangeable around a village square, with trees and shrubs and flower beds. There Mrs. Bun the Baker lived and the Very Reverend Steeple. She

---

'A West Coast magazine was running a series of articles on "home"' and invited me to contribute' (PKP).

Mrs. Bun the Baker ... the Very Reverend Steeple: Mrs Bun the Baker's Wife is a character in the English card game for children Happy Families. The Very Reverend Steeple appears to be the invention of Page's mother.

made up stories about them, or my father did. He was a fine storyteller. And a good reader. On winter evenings around the fire he read me fairy tales from the Brothers Grimm and Hans Christian Andersen. How I agonized for the ugly duckling and, more, much more, for little Kay with a splinter of ice in his heart.

Later, when my brother could sit up and take notice, my parents read to us both – the Doctor Dolittle books, which I am told are now politically incorrect, and the *Just So Stories* of Kipling. Or we played the old wind-up gramophone and listened to Irish songs: 'Cockles and Mussels,' or 'She is far from the land where her young hero sleeps.' And we all sang. Sometimes my mother, in quite a sweet soprano, sang 'The Jewel Song' from *Faust* or sentimental snatches from *The Maid of the Mountains*. And, in the period before we had to sell the piano, my father 'vamped,' a word he used for striking chords that seemed perfectly to accompany any song sung.

In the winter months when theatrical companies from England performed *Peter Pan* or *Charlie's Aunt*, we trailed downtown by streetcar – ourselves and friends of my parents with their children. How chest-bursting our vehement affirmation of a belief in fairies, required to keep Tinker Bell alive.

Winnipeg, with its bare barracks, was a different home. Or rather the props were different. The plot was the same. Now we were old enough to play games in the evening – drawing games and tick-tack-toe, word games and charades. Friends from neighbouring apartments came and

---

He was a fine storyteller: Page arranged for the publication of *Wisdom from Nonsense Land* (Beach Holme Publishing, 1991) a children's book written by her father and illustrated by her mother.
little Kay with a splinter of ice in his heart: a character in Hans Christian Andersen's story 'The Snow Queen'
Doctor Dolittle books ... politically incorrect: The series of books by British author Hugh Lofting, written in the 1920s and 1930s and set in Victorian England, are sometimes criticized for promoting offensive cultural stereotypes.
Just So Stories of Kipling: These stories provide fantastic accounts of the origins of various natural phenomena.
'She is far ... *Mountains*: 'She Is Far from the Land' by Irish poet Thomas Moore, who also set the words to music; 'The Jewel Song,' sung by Marguerite in *Faust* by Charles Gounod; *The Maid of the Mountains*: a musical comedy by Harry Graham and Harold Fraser-Simpson
vamp: 'To improvise or extemporize (an accompaniment, tune, etc.)' (*OED*)

we dressed up. Nowhere was out of bounds when we played: neither cupboards nor drawers. The whole place was grist for the mill of our inventions. And still there was reading aloud.

My father, attempting to draw my attention to my endless chatter, and in the most beautiful gothic script, wrote 'Silence is Golden' in my autograph album – my treasured book with its gilt-edged pages the pale colours of candied almonds. 'I always was behind before but now I'm first at last' someone was sure to write on the first page in a laboured hand.

Among the best of my Winnipeg memories are the birthday parties. Mine. My parents gave wonderful parties. Where wealthy friends may have entertained us by sitting us down to a plate of oysters on the half-shell – a bewildering sight for inland eight-year olds! – my parents had us pinning tails on a donkey my mother had painted, and my father performed magic tricks. One – as beautiful as ballet – consisted of his slow patient filling of a glass with cigarette smoke until it was dense enough to pour like lazy cream into another glass. And, most wonderful of all, performed on the bravest of us, the 'operation,' that made us into babies again. How can I possibly explain this without making it sound macabre or sadistic? It was neither. But it was funny, and at the same time curiously thought-provoking, as if one had truly been taken back in time.

We froze our ears and our noses going back and forth to school in winter and learned to rub the numb parts with snow; fell off roller skates, bicycles and horses; and armed with all manner of potions and incantations to combat ticks, explored the neighbouring woods – fatally dangerous tick territory, according to the lore of childhood.

There must have been bad moments. I don't seem to remember them. And if there were, regular as sunrise, the large brass tray engraved with beautiful foreign writing was set up in the living-room for tea. My mother always put on one cup and saucer more than the number of people she was expecting just in case someone dropped in or I brought a friend home from school. She also cut the thinnest and most delicious bread and butter in the world and each of our successive dogs was taught to 'eat it like a lady,' which meant he must take it bite by bite as one or the other of us fed him by hand.

During a seminal year in England, when I was in my late teens, more or less on my own, the concept of home changed radically. England gave me all the things I had longed for growing up in Canada – ballet, theatre, music, the Blakes in the Tate Gallery. I loved the villages with their thatched cottages, the bluebell woods, the scramble of primroses, the sea. But I was not British, despite my British parents, and England made that clear to me.

Attending the Chelsea Flower Show that brimmed overwhelmingly with beauty – roses the English are so good at, towers of delphiniums ranging from white through all the blues to near-black – it was a prairie crocus that filled me with so great a nostalgia that I had to choke back tears. Even more absurd: I was there in the year of the Silver Jubilee of George V and had been given a seat on the processional route. Never a royalist, I was interested but unmoved by all the crowned heads, and by controversial Princess Marina with whom I sympathized and who, contrary to royal convention, wore a large-brimmed hat that shaded her beautiful face. It was not until Mackenzie King – our black-suited, dumpy little prime minister – drove by in his carriage that I, certainly not a Liberal, barely even political, responded as I had to the crocus in the flower show and was filled by an immoderate nostalgia for Canada. Without my having been aware of the change occurring, that was the moment I knew home now meant not parents so much as Canada, the country where I had grown up.

And so it remained. Until I fell in love.

If one were to conceive of home as a 'nation,' then my track record shows me unreliable, a turncoat unworthy of citizenship. For have I not felt home was New River Beach in New Brunswick, that great stretch of sand where the peaty River New tumbles into the sea; that home was Montreal, as was exotic, tropical Brazil, to say nothing of who knows how many people? Person, place, person, place, person. The one constant, the quality of emotion associated with the concept, the feeling of familiarity or affinity, the sense of belonging.

I have often thought about those who are born and die in the same house. Have they a greater sense of home than I who have moved so relentlessly – changing geography, changing schools or jobs, parting from friends? And what of the nomads of northeast Asia? Does their vocabulary, I wonder, include a word for home? Perhaps the camel train

---

the Silver Jubilee of George V: celebrated in May 1935
Princess Marina: the Duchess of Kent, married to the fourth son of George V

is home, or the vast lands they move across. Or the endless journey itself?

I look up the word 'home' in a dictionary, and the only subsidiary definition that remotely interests me is, 'the objective in various games.' In a flash I am reminded of how HOME meant safety, or the desired goal in tag, hide-and-seek, or prisoner's base, played with neighbouring children on summer evenings as dusk fell; and, later, in the more complicated baseball of my teens. But there were board games where one was sent HOME to start again: a setback and a punishment when one's aim was to move forward and win. And this more negative sense of HOME I now equate with those school friends who had felt imprisoned by the walls of their house and whose parents, in their eyes, were prison guards. For them, home was indeed a punishment, whereas for me, all throughout my school years, because of the love and security my parents provided, home had meant freedom.

Although I was not brought up in the church, some Christian phrases inevitably rubbed off on me, and I recall a moment in middle age when, in another context, the meaning of 'in whose service is perfect freedom' crashed through to me. And as it did, I understood how as a child, in the service of my parents, I was free.

Now in old age, although I have a physical home that I share with someone I love, my sense of home has changed once again. Certainties have gone. I am not as sure as I once was where home is, although I seem to have had glimpses of it. Absurd though it may sound, I feel I am suffering from amnesia – trying to recall something I once knew. Something that has left a trace, neither erasable nor quite legible

And I am reminded of the story from the New Testament Apocrypha, or one very like it, about a child who lives in perfect harmony with his parents. His surroundings are beautiful, as are his clothes. There is no flaw in his life until one day his parents tell him that the time has come for him to go forth on a journey to a distant land and there he must find a jewel and return with it. And so he sets forth to a world that is totally

---

'in whose service is perfect freedom': from the Anglican Book of Common Prayer
the story from the New Testament Apocrypha: Page is summarizing 'Hymn of the Soul' in *The King's Son: Readings in the Traditional Psychologies and Contemporary Thought on Man*, edited by Robert Cecil (Octagon Press, 1980), 5–7, where it is identified as being taken 'with some omissions ... from *The Acts of Thomas* in *The Apocryphal New Testament*, edited by M.R. James' (7).

unfamiliar to him, where he is strangely unfamiliar to himself, where he remembers nothing of his past life, where he doesn't even know there is anything to remember. The food of the country is heavy; it puts him to sleep. So helpless is he, he might be bound hand and foot.

But his parents know the plight of their son and they write him a letter, which, as he picks it up, speaks to him and reminds him of his mission. And so he is able to renew his quest and retrieve the jewel. Whereupon his clumsy clothing falls from him and he puts on his beautiful royal robes again. And then he remembers: he is the son of a king. And when he remembers, he is drawn back to the world of his fathers – realm of dazzling beauty that he knows at last as the place where he truly belongs. Home.

Home. Om. The words are so similar it is hard to avoid thinking of them together. Home – the place to which one belongs: Om – the syllable used in contemplating ultimate reality.

(1999)

Falling in Love with Poetry

I fell in love with poetry before I knew what poetry was. I loved the rhythms and the rhymes. My parents read it to me before I read it to myself. They read me nursery rhymes of course, but my mother had an actor's memory and she knew reams of Shakespeare and Tennyson and Blake. I heard them all when I was a child. I wonder if my parents knew instinctively what respected psychiatrists are suggesting today – that in order to develop the full powers of the mind, early exposure to metered verse is essential. Some go even further and claim that the reading of poetry develops such positive emotions as peacefulness and love.

'Tyger, Tyger Burning Bright' and 'Kubla Khan' crashed through to me when I was about 10 or 12. I had no idea what either of them meant. I had no need to know. I still don't know. Was it AE (George Russell) who said that metrics correspond to something in the soul?

They may well. They certainly correspond to something in the body – lub-dub, lub-dub, the beat of the heart. And I would argue that it is, indeed, the soul that is nourished by poetry unless, that is – unless it gets re-routed to the mind through analysis and amateur psychoanalysis. But I shan't even go there. I don't want to feed the left hemisphere any more than it is already fed by the world we live in. There is a joke – appropriate here, perhaps – of the researcher who said, 'Spiders hear through their legs and I can prove it.' He placed a spider on the table and clapped his

---

'Leslie Eliot, who is the poetry editor at the *New Quarterly*, wrote saying the magazine was doing a series with that title and would I contribute. And I did' (PKP).
AE (George Russell): George William Russell (AE), an Irish nationalist, critic, poet, painter, and mystic

hands. The spider jumped. Then he removed the spider's legs and clapped his hands again. The spider didn't move. 'Proof,' he said.

But back to poetry. Adolescence was time out. It was not that I didn't read but I read what I would now consider lesser poetry: Edna St. Vincent Millay, Samuel Hoffenstein and Dorothy Parker – emotional, humorous, cynical, or world weary.

And then in my late teens I emerged from the poetic shallows. Hopkins' 'The Leaden Echo and The Golden Echo' kindled a coal in me. It was language I loved, not meaning. I liked poetry better when I wasn't sure what it meant. Eliot has said that the meaning of the poem is provided to keep the mind busy while the poem gets on with its work – like the bone thrown to the dog by the robber so he can get on with *his* work. Borges, when asked to read some of his poetry to a class of American students, said he would read it in Spanish. And that those who didn't know Spanish would possibly get more out of it than those who did. People go ape when I say these things.

I found myself increasingly aware of technique: metaphor; the slant rhyme of Wilfred Owen; or expectation met through true rhyme; alliteration, assonance.

> Until that one loved least
> Looms the last Samson of your zodiac.

But I am ahead of myself. I had not yet read Dylan Thomas.

The Canadian poetry I encountered during my school years left me unmoved: Drummond, Bliss Carman, Sir Charles G.D. Roberts, Marjorie Pickthall, E. Pauline Johnson. But in the late 30's *New Provinces* appeared and introduced me to Finch, Kennedy, Klein, Pratt, Scott and Smith. These were our modernists and I read them with a rush of pleasure, greatly encouraged to learn that, in addition to Kay Smith and myself, there were other and more accomplished Canadians writing away.

By now I was in it up to my neck. Over my head. Emily Dickinson, Donne, Yeats, Auden, Lorca, Rilke. The list could go on and on. Wallace

---

Edna St. Vincent Millay: American lyrical love poet; Samuel Hoffenstein: American screenwriter and writer of light verse; Dorothy Parker: American poet and short story writer, known for her sharp wit

Until that ... your zodiac: from Dylan Thomas's 'Deaths and Entrances'

Stevens, Elizabeth Bishop, Ted Hughes. Such different voices. Such varieties of beauty!

In Kathleen Raine's remarkable book, *Defending Ancient Springs*, one of the chapters is called 'The Use of the Beautiful.' The phrase astonished me when I first read it. Does beauty have a use? Goethe says yes in a rather circular fashion: 'The beautiful is a manifestation of secret laws of Nature, which, but for this appearance, had been forever concealed from us.' But how define the word? It has to be broad enough to embrace Aztec art and the art of Islam, the Willendorf Venus and the Venus de Milo. A big stretch!

Is beauty a reminder of something we once knew, with poetry one of its vehicles? Does it give us a brief vision of that 'rarely glimpsed bright face behind / the apparency of things'? Here, I suppose, we ought to try the impossible task of defining poetry. No one definition will do. But I must admit to a liking for the words of Thomas Fuller, who said: 'Poetry is a dangerous honey. I advise thee only to taste it with the Tip of thy finger and not to live upon it. If thou do'st, it will disorder thy Head, and give thee dangerous Vertigo's.'

(2005)

Goethe ... concealed from us.': See note on 'Goethe ... concealed from us."' (p. 21).
'rarely glimpsed bright face behind / the apparency of things': from 'The Filled Pen' (*HR* 1: 210)
Thomas Fuller: seventeenth-century British clergyman, historian, and wit

Had I Not Been a Writer, What Would I Have Been?

Would? Or could?

I probably *could* have been some kind of a gymnast or acrobat because of the way I was glued together – very loosely at the hinges. The additional requirements for success, however, such as dedication, discipline, and desire, were in short supply. The only use to which I put my ability to do the splits, high kicks, sudden controlled falls and a contorted and impossibly sinuous climb over and through a horizontally held broomstick, was to show off at parties.

I might also have been a botanical or medical illustrator, had I followed my love for a fine nib, to trace the delicacies and detailed intricacies of cells. But the page didn't turn that way. Or I didn't turn it. Chance, surely, is a major player. And chance led me early, if indirectly, to theatre, ballet, art galleries, libraries. In the late 20's and early 30's there was no ballet in Canada anywhere, let alone in the Calgary where I lived; art galleries were in short supply, and the only theatrical performances I saw were thanks to British touring companies, and local amateur theatre groups. But there was a Carnegie Library which contained in addition to novels and poetry, books about ballet (oh, fabulous Nijinsky! pale Pavlova's dying swan!); and art books with reproductions, mainly of the old masters, although I vividly remember a book from its shelves introducing me to Epstein. And there were plays.

I was tirelessly and tiresomely in love with the arts. I bored any possi-

---

Brick Magazine asked various writers to answer this question.
Epstein: See note on 'Epstein's *Rima* ... Leicester Gallery' (p. 9)

ble boy friends to death by talking of Chekhov, Shaw, Van Gogh, or by not talking about them and so having nothing to say. And I was writing, but never with the intention somehow of *being* a writer. If not a writer then what did I think I might be? An actor, perhaps? My memory for words was good and I was stage-struck enough for two. But it wasn't really acting itself so much as the literature of the theatre that I loved. Frivolous though I was – and I *was!* – I didn't want to act just any old part. My dream was to play Lady Macbeth or nothing. I was a first class snob. But I was also a lay-about. It didn't really occur to me to be *anything*.

I was well into my twenties when I heard the word anthropology for the first time. Although I was already used to the idea of examining a psyche – did I not have friends absorbed in their analysis! – the idea of examining a culture – even the idea that there were cultures different from the western one in which I had grown up – was an astonishing thought. This cannot be strictly true. Through Gauguin and Van Gogh, Dickens and Tolstoy, I knew something about Tahiti and Russia and Europe. But these were cultures seen through the eyes of painters and writers – works of art, not scientific studies.

It was Ruth Benedict who smashed the plate-glass of my inherited preconceptions. Why had I not known earlier, I railed, as I read *Patterns of Culture*, that such a discipline as anthropology existed? I could then have had it as a possible option, I told myself – ignoring the fact that I had never actually addressed any options at all. There was a fair amount of romanticism as well as dishonesty in my toying with the thought *after* the event that, had I but known, I might have been an anthropologist. I suppose I saw myself living in exotic surroundings and recording an infinity of small details which, in their aggregate, would have added up to some large and original world view. Discomforts, dysentery, despair did not enter into my picture of the anthropologist in the field.

Examining this idea of anthropology some fifty years later and considering the possibility of my having become an anthropologist, I realize how much I have changed. Has physics not taught us that the observer alters the thing observed? And if we need a poet for support, who was it –

Ruth Benedict ... *Patterns of Culture*: *Patterns of Culture*, by American anthropologist Ruth Benedict, supported the concept of cultural relativism by describing behaviours that were said to appear in all cultures.

Karl Shapiro? Peter Viereck? – who wrote, 'The camera photographs the camera man.' In addition, our world has been altered not only by the work of earlier anthropologists who provided us with information about other cultures, but by our actual experience of it through our travels abroad and our immigration policy at home.

What probably fired my early interest was my insatiable appetite for the unfamiliar. That is still intact. But does it give me the right to study another people? To see *their* mote through the beam in *my* eye? Why, I wonder, do we think we are entitled – or qualified – to examine other cultures in the name of science? And if we really are so skilled, why have we not turned this scrutiny on ourselves? Does our own culture not bear looking at? Or are we, in fact, doing just that and calling it sociology?

At any rate I didn't become an anthropologist. And somehow, willy-nilly, despite my lay-about proclivities, I have become a writer, a loner. And I am glad. Almost all groups, if you think about it, become clubs, acquire a jargon, are expected to conform: big business, the services, academe, the church. I cannot believe anthropology is an exception and I have never sought membership in any club.

As to the other possibilities, had I had the discipline to be a gymnast, my life would be over. Had I become an illustrator I would probably be blind. Had I gone onto the stage – short of having become famous – I would now be unemployed.

Clearly I made the best possible choice for myself. Maybe I was prescient. If that is the case, perhaps I could have been a fortune-teller.

(1994)

Karl Shapiro ... Peter Viereck: modern American poets
To see *their* mote through the beam in *my* eye?: 'And why beholdest thou the mote that is in thy brother's eye, but considerest not the beam that is in thine own eye?' (Matthew 7: 3)

Questions and Images

The last ten years span three distinct places – and phases – in my life: Brazil, Mexico, Canada, in that order. All countries of the new world.

Brazil pelted me with images. Marmosets in the flowering jungle; bands of multi-coloured birds moving among the branches of the kapok tree outside the bedroom verandah; orchids in the kapok tree, cucumbers in the kapok tree, the whole tree bursting into cotton candy. Flamboyantes in flaming flower against the sky as one lay on one's back in the swimming pool. Doric palms waving green plumage, growing antlers and beads. Cerise dragon flies. Butterflies as large as a flying hand and blue, bright blue.

Drums from the *favelas* beat like one's own blood, accompanied by the deep bass viol of frogs in the lotus pond; volleys of rockets shattered the black night air, air wet as a sheet and rank with the smell of decaying jackos. Insistent, less obtrusive, the tiny fret of tropical vegetation, the sibilance of bamboos.

Churches, golden as the eye of God, were so miraculously proportioned that one wondered if proportion alone might actually alter consciousness. Enormous quantities of gold leaf. Entire interiors of it, changing space, vibrating strangely; at one moment flashing to blind you, at another reverberating on and on like a golden gong. Moorish designs in tiles and lattices created infinities of intricate repetition.

'George Woodcock when he was editor of *Canadian Literature* solicited articles for an issue he was doing on autobiography. I told him I couldn't do what he asked but contributed these two pieces ["Questions and Images" and "Traveller, Conjuror, Journeyman"] which he used' (PKP).

My first foreign language – to live in, that is – and the personality changes that accompany it. One is a toy at first, a doll. Then a child. Gradually, as vocabulary increases, an adult again. But a different adult. Who am I, then, that language can so change me? What is personality, identity? And the deeper change, the profounder understanding – partial, at least – of what man is, devoid of words. Where could wordlessness lead? Shocks, insights, astounding and sudden walls. Equally astounding and sudden dematerializations; points of view shifting and vanishing. Attitudes recognized for what they are: attitudes. The Word behind the word ... but when there *is* no word ...?

('Why did you stop writing?' 'I didn't. It stopped.' 'Nonsense, you're the master.' 'Am I?') Who would not, after all, be a poet, a good poet, if one could choose? If one could choose. Most of one's life one has the illusion of choice. And when that is removed, when clearly one cannot choose ... Blank page after blank page. The thing I had feared most of all had happened at last. This time I never *would* write again. But by some combination of factors – coincidence, serendipity – the pen that had written was now, most surprisingly, drawing. ('Why did you start drawing?' 'I didn't. It started.' 'But why start something you know nothing about and chuck up all the techniques and skills ...?') Why, indeed, why?

What was that tiny fret, that wordless dizzying vibration, the whole molecular dance? Is that what Tobey's white writing wrote? What was that golden shimmer, the bright pink shine on the anturias, the delicately and exactly drawn design of the macaw's feathers? Why did I suddenly see with the eye of an ant? Or a fly? The golden – yes, there it was again – web spun by the spider among the leaves of the century plant? Surely the very purpose of a web demands invisibility? Yet this was a lure, a glistening small sun, jeweled already with opalescent victims. Victims of what?

Tobey's white writing: Mark Tobey, an American painter whose white writing paintings consist of networks of white lines covering the surface of the work. He was influenced by the ink brush work in Chinese and Japanese painting.

The golden ... Victims of what?: Page refers to this golden web on several occasions. It is the subject of two poems: 'Teia de ouro,' which she wrote in Portuguese and delivered to the Academia Brasileira de Letras (Brazilian Academy of Letters) in Rio de Janeiro on 12 May 1958 (Library and Archives Canada, Page fonds, box 17, file 14), and 'Fly: on Webs,' first published in 1981 in *Evening Dance of the Grey Flies*, 28 (HR 1: 177). She also describes it in *Brazilian Journal* 52, and in 'Ah, by the Golden Lilies' in *Journal of Canadian Studies* 38 (Winter 2004): 191.

The impotence of a marmoset in a rage, pitting itself against me, its fingers like the stems of violets, unable to break the skin of my hand. How quickly one learns about scale with a marmoset for companion. Man in a rage with his gods, or, equally superficially, pleased with them. The glorious macaw, the flesh of his Groucho Marx face wrinkled and soft, his crazy hilarious laughter and low seductive chuckles making him kin until one looked into his infinitely dilatable eye and was drawn through its vortex into a minute cosmos which contained all the staggering dimensions of outer space.

I wonder now if 'brazil' would have happened wherever I was. As to where it pointed I hadn't the least idea, nor, I think, did I ask any questions beyond the immediate ones. But I drew as if my life depended on it – each tile of each house, each leaf of each tree, each blade of grass, each mote of sunlight – all things bright and beautiful. If I drew them all ...? And I did. Compelled, propelled, by the point of my pen. And in drawing them all I seemed to make them mine, or make peace with them, or they with me. And then, having drawn everything – each drop of water and grain of sand – the pen began dreaming. It began a life of its own.

Looking back with my purely psychological eye through the long clear topaz of that day, I appear as a mute observer, an inarticulate listener, occupying another part of myself.

If Brazil was day, then Mexico was night. All the images of darkness hovered for me in the Mexican sunlight. If Brazil was a change of place, then Mexico was a change of time. One was very close to the old gods here. Death and the old gods. Their great temples rose all around one. Temples to the Sun. Temples to the Moon.

Objects dissolved into their symbols. All the pyramids and stairs, plumed serpents in stone, masks of jade, obsidian knives, skulls of crystal – or sugar.

In the rain forest stood the bone-white ruins of buildings – tangible remains of a whole mythology. Buildings so intricate – (tarsal, metatarsal) – one was tempted to believe they were skeletons from which the flesh had

---

macaw ... vortex: Compare 'attention's funnel – / a macaw's eye – contracts, / becomes a vortex' ('After Donne' [HR 1: 225])

skulls of crystal – or sugar: crystal skulls have been discovered by archaeologists in Mexico and Central and South America; sugar skulls are part of the Días de los Muertos (Days of the Dead) celebrations in Mexico.

long since rotted. Motionless. Beautiful. Great ivory kings and queens beneath their lacy cranial combs. Palaces and gardens of the Sleeping Beauty.

The villages seemed unchanged since the beginning of time. The same adobe huts, the same fields of maize, the same ancient languages of clicking consonants, and surely, the same gods. Gods hungry for human blood. (Too much Lowry and Lawrence?) The plazas of Catholic churches were stages for the old rituals of costumed dances, stamped out to the music of conch shell and drum.

In Oaxaca the women of Yalalag wear triple crosses which led Cortes' priests to the mistaken belief that Christian missionaries had preceded them. Oaxacans perhaps understand the symbolism of the cross: time passing, time eternal – 'the intersection of this world with eternity.' In Chichen Itza the Caracol or Snail – an observatory dome from which the Mayans probed the heavens – has four small openings exactly pointing to the cardinal directions. Temples of the Cross. Temples of the Foliated Cross.

Coming as I do from a random or whim-oriented culture, this recurrence and interrelating of symbols into an ordered and significant pattern – prevalent too in the folk arts of pottery and weaving – was curiously illuminating. One did not feel restricted by the enclosed form of the 'design'; rather, one was liberated into something life-giving and larger. I could now begin to understand how the 'little world is created according to the prototype of the great world.'

Great or little, for me it was still a night world – one into which the pattern was pricked like a constellation – bright, twinkling, hard to grasp, harder still to hold. A dreaming world in which I continued to draw and

---

Lowry and Lawrence: references to *Under the Volcano* by Malcolm Lowry and *The Plumed Serpent* by D.H. Lawrence, both set in Mexico

'the intersection ... eternity.': The source of this quotation has not been identified, but it expresses a commonplace in Christian thought dating back to the early Church fathers, such as St John Damascene.

Chichen Itza the Caracol or Snail: The Chichen Itza are ruins located between Cancún and Mérida; the Caracol, or Snail, is so called because of its curved inner stairway.

Temples of the Foliated Cross: located in the Mayan centre Palenque in Chiapas, Mexico

'little world ... great world.': from *The Emerald Tablet*, attributed to the mythical Hermes Trismegistos; one of the key alchemical texts

Great or little ... to dream: Compare 'so dream my / constellation first / and then / casting its pinpoint / dream my star / beambright / a burning glass / can focus and make dance / a dot of light / waiting to be dreamed' ('Waiting to Be Dreamed' [HR 2: 151]).

to dream. How to make a noumenal doll; how to fly; the man with one black and one white hand – (Hari-Hara?); Osiris – (The Seat of the Eye); the room with the invisible walls; the circular dance beside the sea – (Initiation? Into what? A non-religious Christian? A religious non-Christian?) Poetry was more than ever now in the perceiving. My only access to it was through the dream and the drawing.

I had my first two shows during this period. The age of my graphic innocence was past. I had acquired another mask, another label. Each additional one seemed to move me further from my own centre. I was now suddenly and sharply reminded of the young Rilke, bored on a rainy afternoon, coming upon the clothing and paraphernalia of disguise in the wardrobes of a spare room; and how, masked, turbaned and cloaked, he had struck a pose before a mirror. 'I stared' he wrote, 'at this great, terrifying unknown personage before me and it seemed appalling to me that I should be alone with him.'

Which is the mask and which the self? How distinguish, let alone separate, two such seemingly interpenetrating matters? As if pursued by the Hound of Heaven I raced back and forth among the *Collected Works* of Jung, *The Perennial Philosophy*, *The Doors of Perception*, Zen, C. S. Lewis, St. John of the Cross.

---

noumenal doll ... the man with one black and one white hand ... the room with the invisible walls: These are all from Page's dreams (e-mail from Page, 15 December 2005); black and ... white ... (Hari-Hara?): Hari-Hara is a Hindu god combining Vishnu (Hari), who is white, and Siva (Hara), who is black; Osiris – (The Seat of the Eye): Osiris was the Egyptian god of rebirth; his name means 'the seat of the eye.'
the circular dance beside the sea: Compare 'Another Space,' beginning 'Those people in a circle on the sand' (*HR* 2: 170–1).
first two shows during this period: Picture Loan Society, Toronto, Ontario, 23 April – 6 May 1960; Galería de Arte Mexicano, Mexico, 3–24 April 1962
young Rilke ... alone with him.': from *The Notebook of Malte Laurids Brigge*, translated by John Linton (Hogarth Press, 1930), 100–1
the Hound of Heaven: title of a long poem by Francis Thompson describing a sinner relentlessly pursued by God
Collected Works of Jung: *The Collected Works of C.J. Jung* (Routledge & Kegan Paul; Princeton University Press, 1953–67)
The Perennial Philosophy: the concept, first formulated by Gottfried Leibniz, that there is common world view underlying all religions and all forms of mysticism. It was popularized in a book by Aldous Huxley with this title.
The Doors of Perception: book by Aldous Huxley describing his experiences when taking mescaline

> See how he who thinks himself one is not one, but seems to have many personalities as he has moods.
>
> Understand that thou thyself art even another little world, and hast within thee the sun and the moon, and also the stars ...

I began to suspect, in what would once have been near-heresy, that drawing and writing were not only ends in themselves, as I previously thought, but possibly the means to an end which I could barely imagine – a method, perhaps, of tracing the 'small design.' And the very emergence of these ideas began to clear a way, remove the furniture and provide a new space.

But when something one has thought opaque appears translucent, transparent even, one questions whether it might not ultimately become entirely invisible. Solid walls dissolved disconcertingly into scrims. For the moment I was uncertain where to lean.

The dark Mexican night had led me back into myself and I was startlingly aware of the six directions of space.

A day and a night had passed. My return to Canada, if the pattern continued, should be the start of a new day.

The culture shock of homecoming after many years abroad is even greater, I think, than the culture shock of entering a new country. One returns different, to a different place, misled by the belief that neither has changed. Yet I am grateful for the shocks. The conditioning process which turns live tissue into fossil is arrested by earthquake. Even buried strata may be exposed.

I had a small retrospective show shortly after coming home, followed by the publication of a book of 'retrospective' poetry. The shutting of twin doors. Not necessarily on drawings and poems but on *those* drawings and *those* poems.

See how ... stars: quotations from Origen, an early Christian theologian
scrims: 'gauze cloth used for screens or for filtering theatrical lighting' (OED)
the six directions of space: the four cardinal points plus zenith and nadir; a widespread concept in Native American cultures; sometimes also associated with the six-pointed Star of David
a small retrospective show: Art Gallery of Greater Victoria, Victoria, BC, 7 December 1965 – 2 January 1966
a book of 'retrospective' poetry: *Cry Ararat! Poems New and Selected* (McClelland & Stewart, 1967)

The questions had now become more pressing than the images. Some of the questions were retrospective: had the move from writing to drawing been a return to the primitive in myself – to the 'first man' of Van der Post? Was it a psychological starting again from the pre-verbal state? If in the life of the individual and the life of the race, drawing precedes written literature, was this step back really a beginning? Certainly the varied scenes through which I had journeyed had provided no lack of subject matter.

More urgent, however, were the questions raised by Alan McGlashan: 'Who or what is the Dreamer within us? To whom is the Dreamer talking?' What, indeed, is this duologue, so like an effortless poem? Can projected images be manifested as dreams? Are all dreams projected? Or some? Is the Dreamer active or passive? Initiator or recipient? Sometimes one, sometimes the other? And what about the waking Dreamer? Are thoughts the invisible dreams of a daylight world? Projected by what, or whom? Jung's collective unconscious? Al-Ghazali's angels?

I don't know the answers to these questions but merely posing them moves more furniture. I begin to sense another realm – interrelated – the high doh of a scale in which we are the low. And in a sudden and momentary bouleversement, I realize that I have been upside down in life – like a tree on its head, roots exposed in the air.

The question of the mask which confronted me with such violence in Mexico has subtly shifted. In our popcorn packages when I was a child, along with the tin rings, jacks, marbles and other hidden surprises, one was occasionally lucky enough to find a small coloured picture complete with strips of transparent red and green celluloid. The picture, viewed alone, was of a boy with an umbrella and a dog. Seen through the green filter, the umbrella disappeared. The red filter demolished the dog. My subconscious evidently knew something about the tyranny of subjectiv-

---

'first man' of Van der Post: Laurens van der Post, an Afrikaner author and associate of Carl Jung, wrote about the Kalahari Bushman, whom he saw as representing the 'first man' in tune with his own nature and with nature as whole.
Alan McGlashan: 'Who or what ... Dreamer talking?': McGashan is a British psychiatrist. The quotation is from *The Savage and Beautiful Country*.
Al-Ghazali: Sufi mystic, theologian, and philosopher. He argued that all our actions are the results of choices made by God through his agents, the angels.
a tree ... exposed in the air: The image of human beings as an inverted trees goes back at least to Aristotle. It is a commonplace in alchemical and kabbalistic texts.

ity years ago when it desired to go 'through to the area behind the eyes / where silent, unrefractive whiteness lies.' I didn't understand the image then but it arrived complete. It was not to be denied even though only half-glimpsed, enigmatic. It is pleasant now to know what I was talking about!

Whether or not the handful of poems written recently means that writing has 'started' again, I do not know; whether there is an advance over earlier work, I shall have to let others decide. For the time being my primary concern is to remove the filters.

Meanwhile the images have begun again and the questions continue.

'What do I sing and what does my lute sing?'

(1969)

'through to the area ... whiteness lies': from 'Stories of Snow' (HR 1: 153–4), first published in *Poetry* (Chicago) 66, 5 (August, 1945): 238–40
'What do I sing and what does my lute sing?': Page identifies Idries Shah as the source of this quotation (e-mail, 15 December 2005).

Traveller, Conjuror, Journeyman

Connections and correspondences between writing and painting ...
    The idea diminishes to a dimensionless point in my absolute centre. If I can hold it steady long enough, the feeling which is associated with that point grows and fills a larger area as perfume permeates a room. It is from here that I write – held within that luminous circle, that locus which is at the same time a focussing glass, the surface of a drum.
    As long as the tension (at/tention?) is sustained the work continues ... more or less acute.
    What is art anyway? What am I trying to do?
    Play, perhaps. Not as opposed to work. But spontaneous involvement which is its own reward; done for the sheer joy of doing it; for the discovery, invention, sensuous pleasure. 'Taking a line for a walk' manipulating sounds, rhythms.
    Or transposition. At times I seem to be attempting to copy exactly something which exists in a dimension where worldly senses are inadequate. As if a thing only felt had to be extracted from invisibility and transposed into a seen thing, a heard thing. The struggle is to fit the 'made' to the 'sensed' in such a way that the whole can occupy a world larger than the one I normally inhabit. This process involves scale. Poem or painting is by-product.
    Remembering, re-membering, re-capturing, re-calling, re-collecting ... words which lead to the very threshold of some thing, some place; veiled

---

'Taking a line for a walk': 'Drawing is nothing more than taking a line for a walk' (Paul Klee).

by a membrane at times translucent, never yet transparent, through which I long to be absorbed.

Is it I who am forgotten, dismembered, escaped, deaf, uncollected?

Already I have lost yesterday and the day before. My childhood is a series of isolated vignettes, vivid as hypnagogic visions. Great winds have blown my past away in gusts leaving patches and parts of my history and pre-history. No wonder I want to remember, to follow a thread back. To search for something I already know but have forgotten I know. To listen – not to but for.

I am a two-dimensional being. I live in a sheet of paper. My home has length and breadth and very little thickness. The tines of a fork pushed vertically through the paper appear as four thin silver ellipses. I may, in a moment of insight, realize that it is more than coincidence that four identical but independent silver rings have entered my world. In a further breakthrough I may glimpse their unity, even sense the entire fork – large, glimmering, extraordinary. Just beyond my sight. Mystifying; marvellous.

My two-dimensional consciousness yearns to catch some overtone which will convey that great resonant silver object.

Expressed another way – I am traveller. I have a destination but no maps. Others perhaps have reached that destination already, still others are on their way. But none has had to go from here before – nor will again. One's route is one's own. One's journey unique. What I will find at the end I can barely guess. What lies on the way is unknown.

How to go? Land, sea or air? What techniques to use? What vehicle?

I truly think I do not write or draw for you or you or you ... whatever you may argue to the contrary. Attention excludes you. You do not exist. I am conscious only of being 'hot' or 'cold' in relation to some unseen centre.

Without magic the world is not to be borne. I slightly misquote from Hesse's 'Life Story Briefly Told.' A prisoner, locked in his cell, he paints all the things that have given him pleasure in life – trees, mountains, clouds. In the middle of his canvas he places a small train, its engine already lost in a tunnel. As the prison guards approach to lead Hesse off to still further

---

Hesse ... with the picture': from 'A Life Story Briefly Told,' in *Autobiographical Writings*, edited with an introduction by Theodore Ziolkowski, translated by Denver Lindley (Farrar, Straus and Giroux, 1972), 61–2

deprivations, he makes himself small and steps aboard his little train which continues on its way and vanishes. For a while its sooty smoke drifts from the tunnel's mouth, then it slowly blows away and 'with it the whole picture and I with the picture.'

Magic, that Great Divide, where everything reverses. Where all laws change. A good writer or painter understands these laws and practises conjuration.

Yes, I would like to be a magician.

One longs for an art that would satisfy all the senses – not as in opera or ballet where the separate arts congregate – but a complex intermingling – a consummate More-Than. This is perhaps just another way of saying one longs for the senses themselves to merge in one supra-sense.

Not that there aren't marriages enough between the arts – some inevitably more complete than others. But no *ménage-à-trois*. Let alone four or five.

Trying to see these categories and their overlaps in terms of writing and painting I start a rough chart:

WRITING   WRITING/PAINTING   PAINTING

Aural	*Visual*	*Marriage*	*Calligraphic*	*Painterly*
Poetry written to be spoken: Chambers' *Fire*.	Some of Herbert's poems	Arabesques	Klee	Monet etc.
	Dylan Thomas' 'Vision and Prayer'	Concrete poetry	Tobey etc.	
		bill bissett's 'typewriter poems' etc.		
Poetry written to be sung: Cohen's 'Suzanne' etc.	e.e. cummings etc.	Illuminated Ms.		

Chambers' ... Klee: Jack Chambers was an artist in London, Ontario; he did a tape called *Fire* (e-mail from Page, 15 December 2005). George Herbert's 'hieroglyphic' poems 'Altar' and

I get only so far when I stop. Too many ideas rush at me. The categories shift and merge in such a way that I am at times unable to distinguish even between the visual and the aural. Jack Chambers' recording of his poem *Fire* brings me up short. This is an aural poem. It relies for its effect on long silences between words – the silences as significant as the words themselves. If one wants to reproduce this poem on paper one can use the conventions of musical transcription *or* one can so space the words on the page that the poem becomes ... visual. What is time to the ear becomes space to the eye.

'In not being two everything is the same.'

Moving through the category 'Marriage' to 'Calligraphic' and 'Painterly' one must come at length to pure colour. No form at all. And moving from 'Marriage' through 'Visual' and 'Aural' one must finally arrive at pure sound – no words at all.

The notes of the scale: the colours of the rainbow.

'A Father said to his double-seeing son: "Son, you see two instead of one." "How can that be?" the boy replied. "If I were, there would seem to be four moons up there in place of two!"' (Hakim Sanai of Ghazna.)

If writing and painting correspond at the primary level as I believe they do, how and where do they differ?

With a poem I am given a phrase. Often when I least expect it. When my mind is on something else. And my hands busy. Yet it must be caught at once, for it comes like a boomerang riding a magical arc and, continuing its forward path, it will vanish unless intercepted. And that phrase contains the poem as a seed contains the plant. It is also the bridge to another world where the components of the poem lie hidden like the

---

'Easter Wings' mimic the shapes identified in their titles. Dylan Thomas's 'Vision and Prayer' is laid out in a diamond shape, the first and last lines consisting of only one word. bill bissett's 'typewriter poems' are published exactly as produced on a typewriter; compare Page's 'Airport Arrival,' 'Morning,' and 'Skyline' (*HR* 2: 163). The most sophisticated example of 'writing/painting' in Page's work is the title of 'Kaleidoscope' (*HR* 2: 160). Many of Paul Klee's paintings, such as *Child of Woe* and *Death and Fire*, combine painting and calligraphy. Tobey etc.: See note on 'Tobey's white writing' (p. 36).

'A Father ... Hakim Sanai of Ghazna: one of the 'teaching stories' of Hakim Sanai, a Sufi poet, philosopher, and mystic

parts of a dismembered statue in an archaeological site. They need to be sought and found and painstakingly put together again. And it is the search that matters. When the final piece slips into place the finished poem seems no more important than the image in a completed jig-saw puzzle. Worth little more than a passing glance.

Painting or drawing the process is entirely different. I start from no where. I am given no thing. The picture, born at pen-point, grows out of the sensuous pleasure of nib, lead or brush moving across a surface. It has its own senses, this activity: varieties of tactile experience, rhythms. Beating little drums, strumming taut strings. And sometimes there is the curious impression of a guiding hand – as if I am hanging on to the opposite end of some giant pen which is moving masterfully and hugely in some absolute elsewhere, and my small drawing – lesser in every way – is nevertheless related, a crabbed inaccurate approximation.

Yet in all essential particulars writing and painting are interchangeable. They are alternate roads to silence.

(1970)

---

a guiding hand ... hugely: Compare '... the huge revolving world / the delicate nib releases ... / and whatever machinery draws / is drawing through my fingers' ('The Filled Pen' [*HR* 1: 201]).

Afterword to *A Flask of Sea Water*

All my life, I have loved fairy tales. When small, I was lucky enough to have them read to me by parents who loved them too. That was many years before conventional wisdom decreed that they were bad for children – that they were frightening or sad or full of two and three syllable words.

As I grow older I read them less literally and respond to them more deeply. They are tales of hope. They show me unexpected things about myself and the world. They are rich in reminders about perseverance and kindliness. Even more important, they persuade me that another, invisible world can manifest itself within our three-dimensional, daily one.

In the light of all this, it is not surprising that I should want to write a fairy story. But the trouble with a story – as against a poem – is that it needs an idea. Where a poem begins with a rhythm or sound, a story begins with an idea. And not just any old idea – but a charged idea, as evocative as the rhythm that starts a poem. Had I been strong on such ideas, I might have been a fiction writer. As it is, I have always had to wait patiently for any that have come my way. And it is the idea or *occurrence* behind this fairy story that I want to tell you about today. But first, I must give you a brief summary of the story itself.

It begins when a goatherd falls in love with a Princess as she rides by in her carriage. (Rationalists will tell you there is no such thing as love at first sight. But then, fairy tales are not for rationalists.) Poor goatherd! Obsessed now, and unable to think of anyone but the Princess, he leaves his mountain village in the hope of seeing her one more time. Arriving in the capital, he learns that she is to marry the man who provides the King with a flask of sea water. Not a very difficult task, you will say. But this is a landlocked Kingdom where none but members of the Royal Family has ever seen the sea and where most of the inhabitants don't believe that it even exists. Three suitors set out on the quest: the first is a playboy, whose ambitious father – a variant on the mother, ambitious for her daughter – bribes him with a promise of fast horses; the second – power-hungry – is greedy for the throne; and the third is the goatherd – the only one of the three who loves the Princess 'for herself alone.' Their various adventures with a Wizard, a mouse who knows about time, a genie and a flying goat make up the substance of the story. It is another version of the many-times-told tale of accession to the throne, with – I hope – enough new twists to make it enjoyable and exciting.

Now to the occurrence behind the story. One evening I was thinking idly and for no very good reason, about the phrase 'blue blood.' Webster defines it – and I quote – as 'membership in a noble or socially prominent family'; Brewer's *Dictionary of Phrase and Fable* claims – and I quote again – that it 'originated from the fact that the veins of the pure-blooded Spanish aristocrats, whose race had suffered no Moorish admixture, were more blue than those of mixed ancestry.' 'Blue blood' – *sea-blue blood*, so my idle thoughts ran. But, of course! 'Blue blood' had nothing to do with class or race. It was a term applied to the wise, to those who, symbolically, had been to the sea – to that mythical source of all life, the 'great mother,' which, in most cultures, symbolizes wisdom, wholeness, truth. And as for Royalty being 'blue blooded' – (royal blue, note!) – did it, in some Golden Age, have nothing to do with lineage and everything to do with wisdom – just as the fairy tales tell us? The old King, seeking his successor, has to find a young man as wise or, in my terminology, as 'blue blooded' as he. I can't think of a single tale in which the Kingdom *automatically* goes to the rightful heir.

But I am no scholar. I am no etymologist either and I am not trying to persuade you of the rightness of my notion. Nor am I a historian. Perhaps there was no Golden Age when kings were chosen for their wisdom – perhaps that happens only in fairy tales. But, curiously, checking on four

---

for herself alone: 'Never shall a young man ... / Love you for yourself alone / And not your yellow hair.' (W.B. Yeats, 'For Anne Gregory')

historically wise rulers – Solomon, Alexander the Great, Charlemagne and his friend Haroun al-Rashid – I found that not one, through *lineage*, had clear title to the kingdom he ruled.

So that is where my ruminations about 'blue blood' led me; and how I came to write a traditional fairy story in which – I might add – the phrase 'blue blood' is never mentioned, but in which a young man, in order to win the hand of the Princess, makes the long and difficult journey to the sea and returns to the Court with a flask of sea water. In so doing, he proves himself a wise and worthy successor to the old King.

(1986)

Charlemagne and his friend Haroun al-Rashid: The fifth and most famous of the Abbasid caliphs, Haroun al-Rashid received a delegation from Charlemagane and supposedly corresponded and exchange gifts with him.

Fairy Tales, Folk Tales:
The Language of the Imagination

The fairy tale or folk tale has come a long way. In one form or another, it has been with us since speech began. In the days – or should I say nights? – before oil lamps, when work stopped with the light, story telling filled the hours before bed for all members of the family.

In the Middle East, since the time of the Silk Route, stories have been a staple of *chaikanas* and *caravanserai*. But in the West, with the dawn of the Age of Reason, such tales were considered beneath the attention of serious adults and so, like naughty children, they were relegated to the nursery. Yet only a century later, they were once again flourishing in Europe. The Grimm Brothers led the way, with monumental German collections – frequently doctored, as we now know, for the Grimms were a puritanical pair. In their eagerness to eliminate all references to sex, they left us mutilated versions of the originals, full of a violence made meaningless when the reason for it had been removed. Norwegian and Russian collections followed almost immediately. And our century saw the distinguished writer, Italo Calvino, edit and retell an exhaustive Italian collection.

Today in almost any library you can find folk tales from China, Japan, Afghanistan, Persia, Arabia, India – whatever country you want to name.

'I was involved with a storytelling group in the 80's and became very interested in the fairy tale as a teaching story. I wrote this for a talk at a children's festival in Vancouver and later, Nanaimo' (PKP).
chaikanas: tea houses
caravanserai: inns maintained for merchants along major trade routes

Random samples will show that categorisation by country of origin is entirely superficial. Folk tales cannot be issued passports – they already *have* passports. They are citizens of the world, changing their clothing repeatedly, donning the costumes of the region they are in.

With the rise of Feminism women took a look at these tales and found them threatening. Were they not sexist? classist? – thought to encourage either passivity or gold-digging in little girls? How else interpret marrying a prince? Because their length didn't fit the school or library period, the tales found disfavour among teachers and librarians. Publishers declared them wordy. And on top of all that, the new morality saw them as too violent. Too violent, indeed! in an age when you have but to switch on TV – but need I go on?

It is not my intention to be critical of those whose point of view is different from mine. I wish simply to draw attention to the fact that fashions come and go – mind-sets change. Now suddenly, miraculously, fairy tales have become not only respectable they are actually fashionable. Angela Carter, A.S. Byatt, Alison Lurie, Ursula Le Guin, Salman Rushdie have written their own modern fairy tales, or edited books of them or written in their support, and along with Marina Warner – apologist extraordinary – they are recognized once more for what they have always been: tales of wonder and change, with meaning for us all, adults and children alike. It has been interesting to see their re-emergence, to see the rise of story-telling groups, to see the stuff of fairy tale invade even the adult movie screen and catch the popular imagination as it did in the award-winning *The Piano*.

Angela Carter: British writer. Her novel *The Magic Toyshop* and her screenplay for *The Company of Wolves* reflect her Freudian approach to fairy tales.
A.S. Byatt: British author. *The Djinn in the Nightingale's Eye* is one of the works in which she draws on fairy-tale motifs.
Alison Lurie: American author, co-editor of the *Garland Library of Children's Classics*
Ursula Le Guin: American author, best known for her fantasy and science fiction, especially the *Earthsea* series. She has also written books for children.
Salman Rushdie: Indian-born British author. His novels draw on fairy-tale motifs, most notably *Haroun and the Sea of Stories*, about a storyteller.
Marina Warner: British author of *From the Beast to the Blonde: On Fairy Tales and Their Tellers*
The Piano: written and directed by Jane Campion in 1993; won an Oscar for best original screenplay

Fairy Tales, Folk Tales

The first movie I ever saw, *The Thief of Baghdad*, was a fairy tale. I suppose it was made for children. I was six or seven at the time and it thrilled me. In it a penniless boy falls in love with a Princess. In despair over his miserable fate he goes into a mosque where the Mulla asks him the cause of his unhappiness. 'I am in love with a Princess,' the wretched boy replies. 'Then you must become a Prince, my son,' the Mulla answers. At the time I didn't understand how such a transformation was possible, but the thought stayed with me and later the penny dropped. I realised the Mulla must have been talking about personal evolution; that I had been exposed to an allegory.

Ours is a literal and realistic age. We seem to have lost the ability to read at the level of allegory. 'Why does the fairy tale Princess always have to be beautiful?' a friend asked me recently. 'Why can't she be like you or me?' For the simple reason that she is not you or me. Never was and never will be. She is an archetype.

When young, I was lucky enough to have parents who read me fairy tales, who loved them too. Now that I am older, I approach the same tales less literally and respond to them more deeply. They are tales of hope. They show me unexpected things about myself and the world. They are rich in reminders about perseverance and kindliness. And, even more important, they persuade me that another invisible world can manifest itself within our three dimensional daily one. Not a new idea, this. What would the Greek myths be, had their gods not materialised in the guise of humans, animals or even plants? But our culture has chosen to forget the fact, overlook it, consider it primitive or nothing but a tale. We must beware of nothing-butters! They will tell us a pearl is nothing but the disease of an oyster.

Despite my love for fairy tales, I never actually thought of writing one. But when, a few years ago, I was possessed of what to me was a surprising thought, about the origins of the phrase 'blue blood' I could see no way of handling it except as a fairy tale. It was summer and I was staying at a lake with grandchildren and I began telling the tale to them. That was how my 'Flask of Sea Water' began. As it unravelled in my head I had the feeling that I was giving thanks to all those readers and writers and collec-

---

The Thief of Baghdad: directed by Raoul Walsh in 1924
blue blood': See 'Afterword to *A Flask of Sea Water*' (pp. 48–50).

tors of fairy tales who had contributed so generously to my life. For this reason I wanted my story to follow the immemorial conventions: to be set outside time and in no particular place; to be peopled by archetypes; with sun, moon, stars and animals playing their rightful roles, in a story essentially no different from all fairy tales: a story of metamorphosis.

Having written one story it never occurred to me that I would write another. But 'A Flask of Sea Water' ended, inadvertently, with a cliffhanger. As the story closed, the wicked magician turned one of the minor characters into a goat. 'But what happened to the goat?' anxious children asked. And I couldn't answer. What happened, indeed? I decided I had better find out. And so I wrote another story, 'The Goat that Flew' which answers the question. And then, to my total surprise, out of the ending of 'The Goat that Flew' emerged yet another story which wrote itself, in a manner of speaking, and I like it best of the three. And that is probably the last, because after all, three is a very nice number. But I can't be sure. Already a young reader, who has read the unpublished third, has asked for 'just one more.'

Dictionaries tell us that the word 'fairy' in 'fairy tales' is derived from the Latin *fata*, the goddess of Fate, so they are not necessarily stories of the 'little people,' but rather of fate, destiny, design, pattern. As oral narratives they have come to us from all times and all nations. The oldest known written story, *Anpu and Bata* – which may go back even further in oral tradition – is to be found in an ancient Egyptian papyrus more than three thousand years old. Its central theme occurs in more than 800 different versions in Europe alone which are told and retold to this day by people who know nothing of its origin.

That is but one example of the mercurial life of stories. They travel. Or equivalencies spring up. Perhaps they travel *and* spring up. Through time, through space. How can it be that the same story is found in Scotland and also in Pre-Columbian America? And what is the connection between the 6th century Welsh *Mabinogion* and *The Arabian Nights*? And Cinderella, our own familiar Cinderella, is only one of 345 versions, including an Algon-

---

Anpu and Bata: a story of two brothers, with resemblances to the biblical story of Joseph, dating back to the nineteenth Egyptian dynasty, approximately 1200 BC

Welsh *Mabinogion*: a collection of stories found in fourteenth-century Welsh manuscripts, though the origins of the stories are much earlier

quin one, according to a Mrs. Cox who, at the end of the 1800's, was still counting.

Fairy tales exist in an extraordinarily wide spectrum of literature: Homer, the Bible, Shakespeare, the legends of King Arthur. If you are interested in a mind-boggling account of the ubiquity of specific tales, get hold of a copy of *World Tales* by Idries Shah. He shows us, among other things, that folk tales continue when nations, languages and faiths have long since died. One cannot help asking what makes them so enduring? What is humanity's need for them? Are we wired for hearing stories? Sir Laurens van der Post in a recent interview when asked why he thought stories were so important to us replied – and I quote: 'I think they are important to mankind because mankind is a character in a story – we're living a story all the time and this story can only be fed and enriched by other stories.' Once upon a time we knew that. I think we still know it in our bones.

The famous anthropologist, Claude Lévi-Strauss, makes the same point. He tells us that despite the widely diverse cultural features found in the different tribes he has studied, their orally transmitted tales show surprising similarities of structure and theme. From this he concludes that the longevity of the great themes indicates how rooted they are in the deepest layers of the human spirit – evidence, also, of fundamental and universal structures of the mind. Myths, he tells us, 'to all appearances creative, spontaneous, bountiful, nevertheless resemble each other' the world over.

So, what are they then, these stories? What do they mean? And how should we read them?

We can read them as straightforward tales, as survivors of ancient religious beliefs, as carriers of morals. Or, we can read them at the psycholog-

---

a Mrs. Cox ... still counting: Marian Roalfe Cox, in *Cinderella: Three Hundred and Forty-Five Variants of Cinderella, Catskin and Cap O'Rushes* (Nutt, 1893)
World Tales by Idries Shah: Idries Shah was a twentieth-century Sufi writer who played a major role in introducing Sufism to the West. His *World Tales: The Extraordinary Coincidence of Stories Told in All Times, in All Places* was published by Harcourt Brace Jovanovich in 1979.
Sir Laurens van der Post: See note on '"first man" of Van der Post' (p. 41).
Claude Lévi-Strauss: leading French anthropologist, one of the founders of structuralism

ical level – Bruno Bettelheim interprets them in Freudian terms, Joseph Campbell in Jungian! Both arrive at the same conclusion: that folk tales attempt a synthesis – either of the male and female principles as embodied in two characters, or of a vaster scenario involving the animal, vegetable and mineral worlds and the stars in their courses. We can also read them as we might read our dreams – the characters representing the multiple personalities that make up the so-called single self. Interpretations are as varied as are the ways in which people are conditioned. We can read only through our own lenses. But many traditional tales have a surface meaning and a secondary inner significance which, though rarely glimpsed consciously, nevertheless acts powerfully upon us. In the words of Doris Lessing, 'While we are allowing ourselves to be beguiled by the colourful predicaments of princesses, good and bad magicians, and magic horses, something else is working away in our deepest minds.'

That is not to say that the surface meaning is without value. Maxim Gorky is quoted as saying: 'In tales people fly through the air on a magic carpet, walk in seven league boots, build castles overnight; the tales opened up for me a new world where some free and fearless power reigned and inspired in me a dream of a better life.' I have friends who have told me the same thing – friends from broken homes who received comfort and hope from fairy tales when realistic tales of divorce and child custody, offered as consolation, only exacerbated their misery.

As we know from psychology – and here I simplify – the left hemisphere of the brain analyses and the right synthesises. Robert Ornstein, in a recent study, compared the brain activity of subjects as they read two types of material – technical manuals and folk tales. He reported no change occurring in the level of activity in the left hemisphere, but the

---

Bruno Bettelheim ... Freudian terms: a reference to *The Uses of Enchantment: The Meaning and Importance of Fairy Tales* (Thames and Hudson, 1976), in which American psychologist Bruno Bettelheim interprets fairy tales in Freudian terms

Joseph Campbell ... Jungian: Joseph Campbell was an American writer on comparative mythology and religion, influenced by Jung. His best-known work is *Hero with a Thousand Faces.*

Doris Lessing: When British novelist Doris Lessing spoke to the Toronto Branch of the Canadian Club in 1984, Page introduced her as the writer whose 'work means more to me than the work of any other living fiction writer.'

Maxim Gorky: Russian author, journalist, and political activist

Robert Ornstein: American psychologist, who has written a number of books criticizing the dominance of the analytical left hemisphere of the brain in modern society; author of *The Psychology of Human Consciousness* and *The Right Mind: Making Sense of the Hemispheres*

right or synthesising hemisphere was more activated when the subject was reading the folk tales.

Today we live in a left hemisphere society – that is, we are time-oriented, analytical, lineal, rational. Who would deny it? Or, indeed, deplore it? – were it not for the fact that the right hemisphere – the intuitive, image-making, simultaneous, musical hemisphere gets short shrift. I would argue that for the sake of our health – mental and physical – and for the health of our planet, we should be trying to redress the balance of the two hemispheres, using every means available.

A.K. Coomaraswamy writing of tales from the folk tradition says: 'The content of folklore is metaphysics. Our inability to see this is due primarily to our abysmal ignorance of metaphysics and its traditional terms.' And the more familiar Joseph Campbell calls the folk tale 'the primer of the picture-language of the soul.' 'Picture-language.' It is a very interesting phrase. In telling a story, listening to a story, reading a story, one is participating in a picture language – imaging, visualising – employing the right hemisphere. (Imaging, visualising – are these not the words used by holistic healers today?)

For the last word on the subject let me paraphrase Idries Shah. He draws our attention to the fact that we will admit that an orange has colour, aroma, food value, shape, texture and so on. We will readily concede that it may be many different things according to what we observe or need from it. But to the least suggestion that a story has an equal range of possible functions – what Shah calls our 'folkloric evaluating mechanism' – will say: 'No, a story is for entertainment ...' Perhaps we behave this way because our culture has lost a valuable piece of knowledge – the knowledge that by working on a lower level, the level of visualisation – we can put ourselves into a relationship with the higher faculties of the mind.

(1986)

A.K. Coomaraswamy: Ananda Kentish Coomaraswamy, historian and philosopher of Indian art and interpreter of traditional Indi; one of the thinkers associated with the 'perennial philosophy' (see note on *The Perennial Philosophy,* p. 39). The quotation is from 'De la mentalité primitive,' *Études traditionelles,* 1939, 236–8: 278.
'the primer ... of the soul': from *The Flight of the Wild Gander: Explorations in the Mythological Dimension* (Viking Press, 1969), 37
'folkloric ... entertainment': from 'The Teaching Story: Observations on the Folklore of Our "Modern"' Thought' in Robert E. Ornstein, ed., *The Nature of Human Consciousness: A Book of Readings* (W.H. Freeman and Co., 1973), 295

Foreword to *Hologram*

I was introduced to the *glosa* through the ear. Its form, half hidden, powerfully sensed, like an iceberg at night, made me search for its outline as I listened. The eye, of course, sees it at a glance: the opening quatrain written by another poet; followed by four ten-line stanzas, their concluding lines taken consecutively from the quatrain; their sixth and ninth lines rhyming with the borrowed tenth. Used by the poets of the Spanish court, the form dates back to the late 14th and early 15th century. It has not been popular in English.

For some reason I found it challenging – rather in the way a crossword puzzle is challenging. I picked up the first book of poems that came to hand – Seferis, as it happened – in search of four suitable lines. As is often the case at the moment of challenge, everything was easy. Beginner's luck, they call it. Almost without trying, I found the lines that launched 'Hologram.' I won't say I wrote it in a flash, but in a near-flash. The words that controlled the rhymes were *angle, sea, peacock,* and *it*. It was immediately clear that full rhymes would be difficult. Any rhymester knows that English is not Spanish.

I enjoyed the idea of constructing the poem backwards – the final line of each stanza is, in effect, the starting line. You work towards a known. I liked being controlled by those three reining rhymes – or do I mean

---

'Foreword to *Hologram* seemed a necessary introduction to a book of *glosas*, a little known form at the time of its appearance. I was probably urged to write it by Jan Zwicky who edited the book for *Brick Books*' (PKP).
Seferis: 'The King of Asine' by Greek poet Giorgos Seferis.

reigning? – and gently influenced by the rhythm of the original. I felt as if I were hand in hand with Seferis. A curious marriage – two sensibilities intermingling. Little did I then know how obsessed I would become by the form and how, as with all obsessions, it would have to run its course. And little did I know what hazards would lie ahead.

Having completed 'Hologram' relatively easily, it occurred to me that now, towards the end of my life, it would be appropriate to use this form as a way of paying homage to those poets whose work I fell in love with in my formative years. I would pick four lines from Marvell, Blake, Donne, Yeats, Lorca, Rilke, Hopkins, Auden and Eliot and, as it were, 'marry' them. And so I retraced the steps of my early reading – but this time with a different intention. It was a wonderful journey. And full of surprises. I had had so little difficulty with Seferis, it never occurred to me I would run into problems with anyone else. But I soon discovered that border raids were not necessarily going to be easy. Read as I might, I could not find four consecutive lines in Marvell, Blake, Donne, Yeats, Lorca or Hopkins that would 'marry' me.

At first I had no clear understanding of what I needed from the borrowed lines – gradually I learned. They had to be end-stopped, or give the illusion of so being; as nine of my lines would separate them from each other, they had to give me nine lines' worth of space; as well, their rhythm had to be one I could work with, *not* from the level at which one does an exercise – one can do anything as an exercise – but from that deeper level where one's own drums beat. Finally, and vitally, they had to parallel in an intimate way my own knowledge, experience, or – but preferably and – some other indefinable factor I could recognize but not name. Anyone who has ever attempted to match fabrics will know what I mean – it is not colour alone or texture or weight, but all of them in combination. Frequently four lines would meet one requirement but not the others.

For my second *glosa*, 'The Gold Sun' I borrowed lines from Wallace Stevens. They were not enjambed, I was comfortable with their rhythm and, as an additional benefit, the rhyming words were reasonably easy. But I was drawn to them especially because they offered me an opposite

---

Wallace Stevens: 'Credences of Summer'

view from the one expressed in 'A Little Reality' the second section of my poem, 'Kaleidoscope.' Even as I wrote it I knew that Reality is glimpsed not only by addition – courtesy of 'the perfect, all-inclusive metaphor' – but by subtraction as well. Stevens' lines offered me a poem of subtraction – a kind of negative-space companion poem. Would I have thought of it on my own? I wonder.

It was some time before I was able to write a third *glosa*. I searched through Rilke, often so caught up in his poetry that I forgot the purpose of my reading. When I did remember, I was frustrated by page after page of wonderful enjambed verse. At last, in Stephen Mitchell's translation of 'Autumn Day' I found what I needed. Rilke had been one of the overwhelming poets of my youth. His *Duino Elegies* had frequently accompanied me on my way to work by streetcar in Montreal and, more than once, totally engrossed in his images, I had ended up at the car barns. A book of homage would be incomplete if I could not include him.

The poets of my youth were almost all male. Although Marianne Moore had published a *Selected Poems* in 1935 I hadn't read her until much later. But it was unnecessary for me to open her books to know how unaccommodating her lines would be. To find what I needed I had to jump forward in time to Elizabeth Bishop.

I spent a long time on Akhmatova, not yet translated when I was young, but a powerful poetic presence in my later life. Although most adults have suffered some kind of grief or loss, I knew as I read Akhmatova with the intention of selecting four of her lines that the task I had set myself was impossible. How could I accompany her – even in a poem where I was, after all, free to invent?

The real work of writing the *glosas* proved to be this search for suitable lines. 'Work' is hardly the correct word to describe spending the better part of a year reading one's favourite poets but it *was* time consuming. And once having found the four lines, I was not necessarily home free. The losses were almost as numerous as the gains. I began and failed with

---

'the perfect, all-inclusive metaphor': 'A Little Reality,' HR 2: 162
Rilke ... 'Autumn Day': The *glosa* is 'Autumn.'
Elizabeth Bishop: The original is 'Sandpiper'; the *glosa* is 'Poor Bird.'

Lorca, Spender, Jiménez, Hopkins, cummings, MacEwen – for now I was searching beyond the limits I had originally set myself.

'Who were the poets who influenced you?' interviewers often ask and I have always resisted the idea – not that I think my voice so original, but because 'affinity with' seems closer to the truth than 'influenced by.' This year, reading again the giants of my youth, I could not help wondering what their effect on me had been. Had I been influenced by any of them? And if so, how?

Timing is interesting. I had barely formulated the questions before I found what may be their answer in a report by an ornithologist. Attempting to understand how songbirds learn to sing, he brought them up in isolation. To his surprise, they produced a kind of a song – not species perfect, but recognizable. He then introduced them to the songs of a variety of birds *not* of their species and discovered they chose the notes and cadences that, combined with their own attempts, completed their species song. 'Of course!' I thought, 'that is what poets do. We have a song – of a kind. But it is not until we have heard many other songs that we are able to put together our own specific song.'

If the analogy holds, this book contains some – regrettably not – all of the many songs I heard when, falteringly, I was searching for my own voice.

(1994)

Jiménez: Spanish poet Juan Ramón Jiménez. Page eventually wrote a *glosa*, 'Ah, by the Golden Lilies,' inspired by his 'Yellow Spring,' which was published in the *Journal of Canadian Studies* 38 (Winter 2004): 191.
MacEwen: Canadian poet Gwendolyn MacEwen. Page addresses her in 'A Little Reality,' referred to earlier in the essay.

The Sense of Angels:
Reflections on A.M. Klein

Imperial palms, their trunks floodlit, their feathered tops lost in the night sky, could have been free-standing Tuscan pillars. Two rows flanked the courtyard in which an artificial pool, square-cut, flashing darks and lights, reflected fountains and swans. Behind the palms, floodlit too, the pale colonial facades of Itamarity, home of the Brazilian foreign office. Around the pool a studied pattern of small tables, their covers arterial red against the grass. The night air was hot, moist, palpable, rank with the smell of decaying vegetation, sweet with perfume. On the verges of the pool, in groups, and between the tables, men and women in evening dress stood talking, admiring, assessing. Diplomatic uniforms, sashes, decorations; the black and white of tails; coloured silks and satins, diamonds, pearls; all mirrored in the water at our feet. Its mercurial silver-black received and submerged us topsy-turvy among the red tablecloths, the drowned pillars.

We were awaiting the Emperor of Japan. Or was it the President of Portugal?

Drawn together as if from necessity, a young couple and I started to talk; they, newly arrived members of the Israeli Embassy whose previous posting had been Canada.

Did I, by chance, know of the Canadian poet, A.M. Klein?

'I wrote this in response to Joe Rosenblatt's request for an article on Klein for his magazine *Jewish Dialog*' (PKP).
The Sense of Angels: from 'For the Sisters of the Hotel Dieu' (*A.M. Klein: Complete Poems* [CP], edited by Zailig Pollock [University of Tornto Press, 1990], 2: 649)

I did, indeed. Not only of him. I knew him.

Then, undoubtedly I knew he was seriously ill. Nervous breakdown. A grave collapse.

(Abe? Impossible. I, perhaps. Not Abe.) Did they know what had happened?

Canadian anti-semitism. It finally was more than he could bear.

(But we loved Abe! They *must* be wrong. Impossible – his illness; the stated cause. Both impossible.)

The official party arrived, took their places. We too found seats. (Were there not clues in 'Portrait of the Poet?' Yet of all of us on *Preview* – Anderson, Scott, Ruddick, Shaw, and myself – surely Klein – 'and some go mystical, and some go mad' – was the least likely to crack.)

I watched the dancers on the floating stage. Then supper. Brazilian food as prepared for honoured guests is straight out of the Arabian Nights, worthy of Klein's most elaborate metaphors. Their *doces* shining like jewels, unfolding like flowers in baskets of spun sugar, were less than a film before my eyes. Absorbing me, all but tangible – Abe. Abe in a dark suit, eyes twinkling behind ice-cube glasses, reading 'O city metropole, isle riverain!' in a robust baritone. We were in Patrick Anderson's kitchen, I think, crammed around the table, Abe pleased with his 'bi-lingual' poem, savouring its words as he read with a relish, which his recorded version of *Six Montreal Poets* fails entirely to convey.

We were drinking tea – or Anderson was. Tea was rationed still in 1944. Scott would have been drinking the bottle of beer he had brought for himself. (We were modest in our needs and self-sufficient, often going on to Murray's for hot chocolate – a wartime replacement for coffee – or, if too late for Murray's, then to Bowles' with its rubby-dubs and overnight sleepers.) And it must have been summer because the poem appeared in the September issue of *Preview*. So it would have been hot in the flat above the garage – a space not originally intended for man at all – in the

---

'Portrait of the Poet': 'Portrait of the Poet as Landscape' (*CP*, 2: 634–9)
'and some ... mad': from 'Portrait of the Poet as Landscape' (*CP*, 2: 637)
doces: 'sweets' (Portuguese); rich sweets made of flavoured sugar and often combined with fruit or nuts
'O city metropole, isle riverain!': from 'Montreal' (*CP*, 2: 621)
Six Montreal Poets: a recording released by Folkway Records in 1957 of Leonard Cohen, Louis Dudek, A.M. Klein, Irving Layton, F.R. Scott, and A.J.M. Smith, reading their own poetry

lane off Dorchester Street. And the windows would have been wide to let the heat out. Summer dresses and open shirts. So Abe would not have been in the dark suit, which is how I see him in memory's eye. Memory, so faithless to fact, so eager to please and quick to invent.

It was Scott, I suppose who first brought him to *Preview*, for they were old friends. But why he joined us in our last year I don't know. I remember thinking of him as 'old,' probably because he was an established poet with three books of poetry published, because of his rather formal appearance and the orderliness of his life. He was already a partner in a law firm, a husband and father, whereas I led a hand-to-mouth existence, with no fixed address, permanent job, or prospect of marriage. Nor had I possessions in excess of those I could pack into one suitcase, with the exception of a typewriter and – almost irreplaceable during the war – an aluminum kettle, which I carried in my hat box. By actual count, Klein was only nine years older than me and still, everything being relative, a young man. And I remember loving him. Strictly upper torso love. He smiled greatly, warmly, often. He joked in the way poets like best, playing with words.

His poetry had a special meaning for me. I had maintained links with a child's world long after I left childhood – continued to read fairy tales, remembered nursery rhymes with pleasure and amusement, liked riddles, word patterns, tongue twisters. (What after all is a tongue twister but alliteration, pushed past pronunciation?) And here in an established and adult poet I found all these ingredients. He used the vocabulary of the Arabian Nights when he wished, unpatronizingly referred to fairy tales; his Middle Eastern extravagances filled my saddlebags with gold.

It was comfortable to have access to this familiar, sometimes exotic world when I was having to adjust to and contain vital experiences in my emotional life – love and war; and to come to terms with two of the major philosophies of the time – those of Freud and Marx. Iconoclast though I was, neither cap quite fitted. Nor did either system resolve for me the pain of separation and grief or offer satisfying insights into the dilemmas of the heart. Yet in Klein's poetry there was another answer. For all his interest in the immediate world (this was the period of *The Rocking Chair* and political action), for all his acceptance of ideological and psychological

---

The Rocking Chair ... political action: *The Rocking Chair and Other Poems* was published by Ryerson Press in 1948. At this period Klein was deeply involved in politics, as a a candidate for the CCF in the 1949 federal election and as a supporter of the newly founded State of Israel.

theory, he seemed to reach beyond both to a larger reality. And this, though I comprehended it only vaguely, I recognized as real – as a light in the next room is real regardless of whether or not it provides one with illumination. Like a night-light to a child. It glowed reassuringly.

If Klein had religious doubts at this time, a loss of faith even, it did not, I think, affect the religious 'texture' of his work. And it was to this 'texture' that I responded, although it is only now I recognize it for what it is. Does texture in poetry relate to proportion in architecture? The vault of the Cathedral in Bahia, its actual physical shape augmented by areas of gold leaf proportioned to other imponderables – the angle and quantity of light, perhaps – lifted my mind to a different level. I would not have said 'to the contemplation of God,' because such a phrase would have embarrassed me. But it was in such manner that Klein's poetry altered my level of thought. For all its religious imagery I did not see it as religious poetry. For him, yes. For me, no. Had I seen it so, it would have put me off. I saw it as fairy tale, fable, pattern of words. I ate the peach for the taste and it nourished me.

In 'Chad Gadyah' there were nursery rhyme echoes:

The butcher began to kill the ox,
The ox began to drink the water,
The water began to quench the fire,
The fire began to burn the stick,
The stick began to beat the dog ...

But, 'Chad Gadyah' provided what the nursery rhyme lacked – a resolution and a change of level:

In that strange portal whence
All things come, they re-enter;
Of all things God is centre,
God is circumference.

Did 'Once in a Year' not remind me that man is royal even when he forgets he is, in the unreality (unroyalty – it is the same word) of day to

---

'Chad Gadyah' ... 'Once in a Year': sections of 'Haggadah' (*CP*, 1: 128–31), in which Klein describes the Passover celebration

day? And that the very purpose of festival is to liberate the spirit from these bonds. To help man remember.

His 'Biography' recalled a story my grandfather used to tell of the man who, deciding his donkey was eating too much, gradually reduced his ration. When the donkey died the man complained, 'If I'd had just a bit more time I could have brought him to the point where he lived on nothing at all.'

In 'that fabled city' which 'stands in Space's vapours and Time's haze' where once I saw Zion, the socialists' ideal state or individuated man, I now half-glimpse the archetypal city – glimmering, luminous – of which Doris Lessing writes: 'There was no central building to the city, yet the people maintained that somewhere in it was such a lode-place or nodal point – under the city perhaps; perhaps in some small not apparently significant room ... It could have been the common talk about this room was another way of putting their belief that there existed people, in this city, who formed a kind of centre, almost a variety of powerhouse, who had no particular function or title, but who kept it in existence.' The thirty-six men? Rilke's Angels? Ibn al-Arabi's?

Was it Klein who introduced me to Rilke? Probably not. But certainly it was he who, in the bar of the Mount Royal Hotel, read aloud from my copy of the Elegies so that I might hear the sound of them in German. A re-reading of those poems today summons up a kind of cavernous booming of his voice in my ear. We drank together in that bar from time to time and read our poetry to each other and our encounters were easy, sometimes hilarious. Still, I knew him somehow less well than I knew the others on *Preview.* When a member of his family died, although I wanted

---

'Biography': CP, 1: 283–4
'that fabled city ... Time's haze': from 'Autobiographical' (CP, 2: 566)
Doris Lessing ... in existence.' from *The Four-Gated City* (Alfred A. Knopf, 1969), 13
The thirty-six men: According to Jewish legend, the world owes its continued existence to thirty-six anonymous just men who arise in each generation. There is a similar Sufi tradition concerning forty hidden saints, associated with Ibn al-Arabi in particular (see note on Ibn al-Arabi below).
Rilke's Angels: Rainer Maria Rilke's *Duino Elegies* begin: 'Who, if I cried out, would hear me among the angels' hierarchies?'
Ibn al-Arabi: a leading Sufi philosopher. He held that a specific angel acts as an intermediary between God and each individual soul.

to express my sympathy, his bereavement silenced me, locked me into a shyness I would not have felt with the others.

Now in Brazil, his illness placed him further out of reach than when death had struck at his family. Further out of reach, yet near, very near, immanent. I tried to see Brazil with his exuberant exactness. Its baroque flora, the Moorish influence in tile and architecture, the intricate play of light and shadow in the *brise soleils*, the serpentine blacks and whites of its sidewalks became for me an only slightly altered version of his Casablanca: 'this was an art of traceries and fretwork where both space and space filled, combined and embraced, interlaced, wove out of iron or the inscribed stone their flowing arabesques: *Neskhi*, the calligraphy of growing things, pattern of shoot and tendril of climbing vine ... an art of alternations and changes where the white marble gave way to black, the black to white, twins of symmetry in polite accommodating dance ...'

He was of course describing calligraphy, a direction my own pen had taken now that it had turned from writing to drawing, and that I was discovering – contemporary and secular – in the concrete poetry of Pignatari and the two de Campos, as well as in the 'white writing' of Mark Tobey. What more did Klein know about this art? It is, he explains – and he almost describes his own novel – 'a discipline of design ... the artist abstracting ... the beauty of the world to its planes and lines ... eschewing image, delighting in form; *Kufic*, the very pilgrims of the script, staff-bearing, marching; and everywhere through the cursive, which is like a sultan at ease, or through the angular, which is like a sultan in state, filling my soul with remoteness, with remoteness made familiar and near.' Two opposite poles of space, joined to become one through the focus of script.

Miriam Waddington, in her book on Klein, points out that archaic words – frequently used by the young poet – carry 'double time,' 'double

---

'this was an art ... accommodating dance': from *The Second Scroll*, edited by Elizabeth Popham and Zailig Pollock (University of Toronto Press, 2000), 37
Pignatari: Décio Pignatari, associated with the concrete poetry movement in Brazil
the two de Campos: Haraldo and Augusto de Campo, forerunners of the concrete poetry movement in Brazil
'white writing' of Mark Tobey: See note on 'Tobey's white writing' (p. 36).
'a discipline of design ... familiar and near.' *The Second Scroll*, 37
Miriam Waddington ... Klein: *A.M. Klein* (Copp Clark, 1970), 130–1

vision historically'; whereas metaphor, which in his later poems came to replace archaisms, 'also doubles, condenses, and gives two for one; yet its emphasis ... is on meaning.' 'Gives two for one' – gives two *in* one. Two or more separate ideas, objects, images, fuse. In so doing generate energy. Illuminate.

For me, Klein's struggle to overcome duality, to reverse the fragmentation of contemporary consciousness, to make whole, becomes acute in his last book, *The Second Scroll*. Message and method merge, centauresque, to assist him. The theme in itself is two in one – a double hero myth. As Uncle Melech sets out on his quest, dies, and is reborn, so the narrator – the outermost, one might say, in a series of Chinese boxes of which Melech is the smallest – sets out on *his*. By the use of glosses, what might have been a thick book is kept slim. Like an accurate lens-setting they extend the depth of field. Background, foreground are equally sharp. Metaphor, pun, even a return to archaisms are employed to connect and interlink in the convoluted near-symmetry of arabesque the relationships between separate creeds, separate continents, separate spheres.

If, as some modern etymologists say, the word 'religion' derives from 'ligare' ('to bind'), then religion could be said to be a binding together of what is, in reality, bound; of what appears fragmented only when seen through the prismatic eye of unregenerate man. Metaphor, then, becomes religion's handmaiden. And the perfect metaphor would unite all things; leave nothing further to be said – an intimation perhaps of what Rilke meant when he wrote of 'the kind of speech that may be possible THERE, where silence reigns.'

If I could talk to Abe today I would tell him how knowing him, loving him, reading him, formed part of the design that led me to Persian Rumi, poet and mystic; and how reading Rumi has given me further insights into, and greater sustenance from the work of that godly man, A.M. Klein.

(1973)

'Rilke ... reigns.': from *Duino Elegies*, translated with an introduction and commentary by J.B. Leishman and Stephen Spender, 4th ed. (Hogarth Press, 1975), 21

Rumi: Jalal al-Din Muhammad Rumi, one of the greatest Sufi poets

Notes on Re-reading George Johnston

I have your book in hand.
It awes me.

So begins George Johnston's poem 'To Bob McRae on Reading His Book, *Leibniz: Perception, Apperception & Thought.*'

I feel the same way about *Taking a Grip*, the book in which the above extract appears. And because I could not have written those three-stress lines or caught their solemn, teasing tone, I borrow them, not knowing how else to pay so unmawkish a compliment to a writer I admire so greatly.

Bob McRae is the poet's brother-in-law and, since Johnston has abandoned his imaginary beings – Mrs. Murple, Mrs. McGonigle, Aunt Belleek, Miss Knit, *et al.* – he is at his happiest writing about family and friends. (This sounds terrible. It isn't.) Not that he is not 'happy enough,' as he says, with the countryside: bees, pigs, trees, cesspits even.

The poem to McRae evokes utterly serious mirth in us – not at McRae – at Johnston perhaps, at the process of thought, at language –

'The first of these two essays appeared in *Raddle Moon*. The two together appeared in the special Johnston issue of *Malahat Review*. After George's death it was reprinted in *Notes and Queries*' (PKP).
'To Bob McRae ... Thought': *Taking a Grip: Poems 1972–1978* [TG] (Golden Dog Press, 1978): 64–6
Mrs. Murple ... Miss Knit: characters from Johnston's first volume of poetry, *The Cruising Auk* (Oxford University Press, 1959)
happy enough: a reference to *Happy Enough: Poems 1933–72* (Oxford University Press, 1972)
cesspits: 'Taking a Grip' (*TG*, 55)

> Awesome thoughts
>   awesomely thought out.
> Your prose begets
> a rational pleasure
>   that nobbles the old doubt

Nobbles, indeed! Where does he learn these good simple words? In the poem he looks up McRae's 'entelechies'; forgets what it means. I look up 'nobbles'; hope to remember. It is a fine word. Johnston uses fine words, old-fashioned words, archaic words: gambrel, foison, spunk, ruth, curtal, becks.

Fine phrases too. Of a son walking off into distance – 'he dwindles before our pace from which *hurry / has been put by.*' 'I do / almost anything to be outdoors / *when her cheek shows.*' Of bees in their winter hive – 'Between gusts you can hear them / *a bunched hum.*' 'Restlessness is ...' but let us have this poem whole, with its inevitability:

There

One keeps itching to get there. Where? Never mind
where: one gets there at last, and does not come back
again to tell anyone else where
or how, or what it is like there.

One drives internal combustion vehicles
or one walks, or one rockets across the sky.

Nobbles ... becks: These words are defined in the *OED* as follows. Nobble: 'to strike, hit, beat up; to stun.' Gambrel: ('Between,' *TG*, 12): 'the bend or joint of the upper part of a horse's hind leg; the hock'; hence 'gambrel roof,' 'a curved or hipped roof, so called from its resemblance to the shape of a horse's hind-leg.' Foison ('Delay,' *TG*, 30): 'plenty, abundance.' Spunk ('To Bob McRae,' *TG*, 65, 66): 'spirit, mettle; courage, pluck.' Ruth ('Ribs, Roasts, Chops, Bacon,' *TG*, 27): 'the quality of being compassionate; pitifulness; the feeling of sorrow for another; compassion, pity.' Curtal ('Pen Y Maes,' *TG*, 48): 'anything docked, or cut short.' Beck ('Pen Y Maes,' *TG*, 47): 'a brook with stony bed, or rugged course, such as are those of the north country.'
'he dwindles ... *put by*': 'Between' (*TG*, 14).
'I do ... *shows*': 'Luck' (*TG*, 18).
'Between ... *bunched hum*': 'Wintering' (*TG*, 20)
'There': *TG*, 23

> Restlessness is the ness one goes by.
> It infallibly gets one there.

'The ness one goes by.' What a great, long, accompanying promontory. Dear George! There is no one like you.

As we read his observations of everyday, our hoard of subliminal impressions surfaces and becomes conscious, and 'Yes' we say to his crickets and katydids, and 'Of course' we say to his shouldering brooks and wet wheel tracks. We have seen it all once he reminds us, gives us it back.

The writing is as casual sounding as neighbours' talk. But poetry students take note: it is intricate as lace. Look for the rhymes and the half-rhymes – concealed as birds' nests. Listen to the stresses, count the syllables.

If one needs convincing of the masterly control Johnston has over words, what better proof than his translations from the Icelandic of *The Gisli Saga*. The verses which appear from time to time in the narrative are written in court metre. Even to think of it gives one brain fever. But let us think of it.

Each stanza has eight lines – four pairs of lines; three stressed syllables per line, the third always trochaic. The paired lines are linked by alliteration. There is a half-rhyme in the first line of each pair, a full rhyme in the second. Like this:

> I fought a long fateful
> Fight, this was my nightmare;

---

crickets and katydids: 'Delay' (*TG*, 31). shouldering brooks: 'In Spate' (*TG*, 21). wet wheel tracks: 'Short Untitled Unconnected Poems' (*TG*, 29)

The Gisli Saga: the story of Gisli, who is outlawed for killing his brother and hides in northern Iceland until he is captured and killed. See 'The Saga of Gisli,' translated by George Johnston, in *Three Icelandic Outlaw Sagas* (Everyman, 2001).

court metre: See 'George Johnston Reading' (*HR* 2: 129) for a poetic account of court metre. Page was inspired by the reading which she describes in this poem to try her own hand at court metre (a slightly simplified version) in 'Crow's Nest' (*Malahat Review* 67 [February 1984]: 11–12). Johnston responded with 'Crows' (*sic*) Nests (*sic*) in Court Metres,' dedicated to Page (*Endeared by Dark: The Collected Poems* [*ED*] [Porcupine's Quill, 1990], 289).

I fought ... ruddy: *Three Icelandic Outlaw Sagas*, 60

> Single, not soon was I
> Slain by their main power.
> Good flesh by my gashing
> Gave I mouths of ravens,
> But in your white bosom
> Bright blood drops fell ruddy.

Hard enough to compose in this form, to observe such strict rules in so small a space, but how much harder to translate and make beautiful – as this is beautiful – these tight little stanzas.

No wonder he can write a sonnet with no apparent pushing and shoving, so that as one reads one barely suspects its hidden armature. Yet it is this armature, perhaps, that holds and keeps the fragile dust of this poem in suspension:

Cathleen Sweeping

> The wind blows, and with a little broom
> She sweeps against the cold clumsy sky.
> She's three years old. What an enormous room
> The world is that she sweeps, making fly
> A little busy dust! And here am I
> Watching her through the window in the gloom
> Of this disconsolate spring morning, my
> Thoughts as small and busy as her broom.
>
> Do I believe in her? I cannot quite.
> Beauty is more than my belief will bear.
> I've had to borrow what I think is true:
> Nothing stays put until I think it through.
> Yet, watching her with her broom in the dark air,
> I give it up. Why should I doubt delight?

Even in the delight, Johnston strikes a mourning note. It is the voice he uses when he is 'homesick in the world,' when he hears Schubert's

---

'Cathleen Sweeping': *ED*, 25
'homesick in the world': 'Kent Doe's Ordination' (*TG*, 17).

'undernote of thunder' and makes Dooms-day of his daughter's departure by proclaiming '... it is not Doomsday after all, just au revoir.'

He asks difficult, serious questions neither he nor we can answer. He celebrates the world and our comings and goings. He reminds us that we are human and that we can love one another and he rarely forgets or lets us forget 'the big summing up.'

***

How Johnstonian the title – *Ask Again. Home Free, Happy Enough, Taking a Grip, Ask Again* – in that order, almost the story of a life.

Equally Johnstonian the thirty-seven poems in this beautifully designed volume from Penumbra Press: poems for named people – Johnston honours his friendships and kinships; quirky, idiosyncratic poems; acrostics; poems knit from the strict pattern of scaldic verse; poems with cadences that teeter and tilt as delicately as mobiles.

Of the three sections in the book, two – *Friends and Occasions* and *Marriages, Births, Deaths* – contain lamentations for life passing and life concluded and celebrations for life begun. Personal but not private, this is loving, often colloquial, unsentimental poetry. The diction does not permit sentimentality nor, I think, do the rhythms. Both, of course, projections of the man, himself, who knows that

> Márried lífe is whát
> one mákes ít; there's lúck,
>   blíssful tímes – and nót,
>   thín ánd thíck,
>   júst sítting it oút;
>   áll párt of the lífe.
> Máy you máke the lót ...
>   *from* 'A Marriage Poem for Peg and John'

'undernote of thunder': 'The B-flat Sonata' (TG, 17)
'it is not ... au revoir': 'Sue Power and I see Cathleen Off' (TG, 54)
'the big summing up': 'Goodbye' (TG, 61)
Ask Again [AA] (Penumbra Press, 1984)
Home Free: Oxford University Press, 1966
'A Marriage Poem for Peg and John': AA, 37

I have marked the stresses as I hear them – in this case, three to a line. They are always worth paying attention to – for one thing, they tell you how to read the poem. But I have marked them for the purpose of showing that where they fall controls the gait of a poem and how, here combined as they are with whole and half-rhymes, they create an uneven gait, perfectly suited to the subject matter.

Self-indulgence finds no place in Johnston's ironic amusement at the human condition. In 'Love and Marriage,' he marvels:

> How Uncle Fletcher goes
> about love, dear knows.
> He and a someone dis-
> reputable find bliss ...

And in his respectful, admiring poem to Northrop Frye, let us hear how playfully he begins:

> Moncton, did you know
> that in your streets grew
>   Canada's famousest
>   speed typist ...

One might be tempted to surmise, on the basis of the poems from which I have quoted, that his sense of structure and its attendant graces are the result of Johnston's work of translating the intricate verse of the scalds – the court poets of the Viking age; that these skills are a gift, as it were, in return for submitting to so exacting a discipline. But in his poems in *The Cruising Auk*, written before the real work of translation began, we find similar structures and graces. More probable then, that like called to like, that the conjunction arose from affinity.

Let me quote briefly from 'What Do the Scalds Tell Us?' – an article by Johnston which appeared in the *University of Toronto Quarterly* in 1982.

'Love and Marriage': *AA*, 39
Moncton ... typist: 'A Celebration for Northrop Frye' (*AA*, 23)
The Cruising Auk: Oxford University Press, 1959

It will give us a glimpse of his attitude to translation and to his own work.

> What I had done was place first importance on the form. The sense had to realize itself in the form. What I have learned since, gradually – or, rather, *learned over again* (italics mine) – is that this is the most fruitful approach to the composing of my own poetry. I unlearned the dictum that the poem should find its own form. The poem finds its form more surely within a convention than not.

In Johnston's hands, the form invariably draws attention to the language itself. Variations on rhyme and half-rhyme – a requirement of scaldic verse – expose the very skeleton of word sounds; while alliteration – another requirement – sets up a pattern of reverberations. This is aural poetry, indeed, and so should be read aloud.

For all the poetic pleasures to be found in the first two sections of *Ask Again*, it is the third section that pleases me most. Here we see the fine eye Johnston has for nature, here we are treated to the most astonishing of his syntactical singularities, to his most serious play. What to say about a poem like 'Onset'?

> A between time; what's to come
> looms. Let it not loom.
> It has loomed enough.
> Let it, whatever it is, loom off ...

Funny, yes. Darkly funny. The half-rhymes, the short sentences and all those 'looms' conjure and re-conjure the never-written, rhyming 'doom' and lead the reader on from autumn towards a metaphorical and literal winter.

'Onset,' 'White,' 'Spring Chorus' and 'Swept Sky' are the poems I found most moving. It is as if the very constraints he imposes upon himself

---

What I had done ... than not: 'What Do the Scalds Tell Us?' *University of Toronto Quarterly* 52 (1982/83): 3
'Onset': AA, 58
'White': AA, 61. 'Spring Chorus': AA, 65. 'Swept Sky': AA, 59. 'close / stars crowd': 'Frost' (AA, 62)

force something to break loose. There is no compass too small for the big winds and thunder. In even the sunniest poems one can hear thunder in the distance. In even the briefest, 'close / stars crowd.'

Johnston is one of the most finely tuned poets we have – a master watchmaker who can also build Big Ben.

For my next birthday I would like a collected George Johnston – all the poems from his books of poetry and all the translations from the Scandinavian in one great book. It would make a most glorious din.

(1984 and 1986)

Afterword to *The Innocent Traveller*

Twenty three years after the publication of *The Innocent Traveller*, in a characteristically modest letter to John Gray, her publisher, Ethel Wilson wrote: '... It is well written, I like it ... I value it ...'

How different from her doubts in November of 1944 when she first submitted the manuscript to the Macmillan Company:

> Dear Sir – I shall venture to send you a few stories, three of which appeared in the New Statesman and Nation, the fourth in the Canadian Forum, the others not at all ... I send these, not with expectations of acceptance, but with plain humility, as I am not sure whether they are good, a little good, or no good, or whether they would interest a public at all.

Two days later, even less secure, she wrote again:

> Dear Sir – I sent you lately a bundle of short stories which had suddenly begun to burn a hole in my pocket. I think I told you of my own uncertainty as to whether they are at all good.
>
> Distance has, I think, lent a proper perspective, and also the enormous events which agitate the country now. And my stories have dwindled into their proper size – the matter is so trifling, old fashioned, and of personal interest only, perhaps. One can hardly blame a public that requires 'social

---

'*The Innocent Traveller*, *Emily's Quest* and *Nights Below Station Street* were written at the request of David Staines as Afterwords for his New Canadian Library editions of the books by those names' (PKP).

awareness' in its reading, or something truly funny and entertaining – So this leads me to say that when you send me these little pieces – collect – I will welcome them into obscurity again.

Of such confidence and misgivings are good writers made! And Ethel Wilson was a very good writer indeed – a quirky and sophisticated writer with an individual style, tilting and elliptical. Witty as well as funny. Unique. But as yet unproven.

'If you cannot make something out of that Topaz saga you're not the writer we think you are,' read the note accompanying the returned stories. It was not an outright rejection but for Wilson it might as well have been. 'When you definitely refused Topaz for the good reason of being short stories,' she wrote in reply, 'and I definitely knew that I can't and won't change her form, I sent them to ... Simon and Schuster.' And so began the discussions with Macmillan which were to continue over the succeeding five years.

In today's literary climate it is difficult to understand why Macmillan took so long to decide to publish. One feels anyone with half an eye would have jumped at such a book. And it is clear from the correspondence, that Macmillan *had* half an eye. The trouble lay with the other eye-and-a-half which could see a book as a book only if it was a novel. Linked stories, however consecutive, would not do. This attitude was not peculiar to Macmillan. In Canada few collections of stories, other than anthologies, had appeared before the sixties.

Then in 1946 Wilson wrote *Hetty Dorval*. Unarguably a novel, it was published by Macmillan in 1947. Two years later, her first-born, *The Innocent Traveller*, appeared. Wilson was sixty-two years old.

The Innocent Traveller is both family chronicle and fiction. 'The persons and incidents are true' Wilson said of it in 1957, 'or, when I made some up (as I did), they are so truly characteristic of certain persons that they approximate to truth.' And she was right. Her characters *are* true – fictionally true. Flesh and blood.

'One day I will write down my stories,' she is reported to have said to a friend, 'but not until Granny, Aunt Eliza and Aunt Belle are dead.' The last of them, Aunt Eliza, died in 1943, aged one hundred. Wilson must have meant 'publish,' not 'write,' for it is evident from her papers that she had been writing and revising *The Innocent Traveller* (originally called

Topaz) for nineteen years. During that time its title was changed and changed again, as was the order of its chapters. What remained unchanged was Eliza herself, the book's central character, and energy. '... I called her Topaz,' Wilson wrote. 'There had to be a "z" in her name, for she had sudden small dazzles and sparkles, and she was like a semi-precious stone ...'

Let us have a look at Topaz in the book's opening paragraph as she first appears and makes her presence felt:

> Far away at end of the table sat Father, the kind, handsome and provident man. At this end sat Mother, her crinoline spread abroad. On Mother's right was Mr. Matthew Arnold. On each side of the table the warned children ate their food gravely, all except Topaz on Mother's left. Topaz, who could not be squelched, was perched there on the top of two cushions, as innocent as a poached egg. Mother sat gracious, fatigued, heavy behind the majestic crinoline with the last and fatal child.

Already we are caught in the spell of the prose, in the pull of the plot. Who cares if this is fiction or memoir, short story or novel? A world has been created in six sentences. A Victorian world. *Pater familias*, kind, handsome, provident, friend of Mr. Matthew Arnold. Mother about to die. (What a great deal is suggested about men and women of the period. Husbands and wives!) And the warned children – were they indeed not warned in Victorian England? (children who should be seen and not heard – gravely eating their food.) All, that is, except Topaz, impervious then, impervious always, to the limitations and conventions of her narrow world.

In real life, whatever that is, Topaz would drive one to distraction. She is talkative, trivial, tiresome – overwhelmingly unaware of the feelings of those around her. She is one of those unmarried women who stay 'girls' all their lives, who are good sports, game for anything. Chattering and merry. Infuriating. At the same time she is unexpectedly flexible, unwaveringly kind, and, due to an almost total lack of imagination, endlessly surprised by life. She moves uncomplainingly through a hundred years of rapidly accelerating change, from Victorian England to post-Second-World-War Canada, only once raging at her fate.

'I am afraid that if I depart from the life of Topaz as it was' Wilson wrote to her publisher, 'and begin to make a *story*, either rather violent or rather psychological out of it, I have to introduce someone who *does* something to Topaz, or to whom Topaz *does* something. But the point about her, I find, is that having no touch with reality below the top layer, she does nothing to anyone! She is incapable of it.' She is, indeed, the innocent traveller of the well-chosen title.

With such material to work with, why is Topaz so memorable, so endlessly fascinating, so lovable? The answer must lie in the fact that Wilson's inscribing eye – her incising, incisive eye – is sufficiently infused with a loving spirit that we catch her love. Literate Ethel Wilson, master of implication, mistress of delicate balances, is incapable of a boring thought. She carries us lightly, as though bearing no weight at all, through a myriad interweaving mini-stories, deftly skirting the real pain, burning us only a little, but burning us just the same. Letting us touch the flame so we know how it feels. But not dwelling on it anymore than does Topaz herself.

'The drop of water, the bird, the water-glider, the dancer, the wind on the canal, and Topaz, are all different and all the same' she says in the Author's Note. And as this sharp and gentle book unfolds, she shows us their dance – back and forth in time, back and forth again – weaving an intricate fabric into which, while the spell is upon us, we are woven too. We become part of that Victorian community of women – of widows and unmarried aunts; part of that ordered, harmonious world: upper middle-class, reading Greek, travelling abroad, knowing our place. *Knowing our place.* Yet the detached and thoroughly modern mind of the author writes, at the same time, a wry, invisible gloss.

So Topaz, then, is wonderfully drawn, as are the splendid others. And that includes the author herself who appears first, as a disembodied 'I' – surprisingly, before she is even born. Later, as the orphaned, third-person Rose, she adds a younger voice to the Grandmother's house, even though she is usually off in her bedroom, hidden or half hidden, (but observing, observing), while Topaz stamps about centre stage congenitally insensitive to everything – well, almost everything – around her.

But what of the book itself, what of its shape? For it *has* a shape, this collection of stories (or is it a novel, after all?). So delighted are we by its style, by its characters who have become our friends, that we have altogether forgotten shape. We have been carried along – like Topaz herself –

absorbed, unthinking, until towards the end, the book gathers itself together, and we see by its circularity and lift that it is, in fact, a spiral. Echoes of its beginning sound once more, altered as echoes have to be. Topaz speaks poetry again not, as in Chapter 1, *to* Mr. Matthew Arnold but poetry *by* Mr. Matthew Arnold. And as the first poem –

> Two are better far than one
> For comfort or for fight.
> How can one keep warm alone
> Or serve his God aright?

– might anticipate Topaz's single life, so the second anticipates her death:

> A man becomes aware of his life's flow,
> And hears its winding murmur; and he sees
> The meadows where it glides, the sun, the breeze ...
> ... And then he thinks he knows,
> The hills where his life rose,
> And the sea where it goes.

Three short chapters from the end when, as through a scrim, we glimpse the brutalities of war, Wilson suddenly confronts us with what previously she has repeatedly hinted at – the enigmatic nature of time – and which we now see as the theme of the book. 'The future,' she tells us, '[is] really one with the present and the past.'

And as we confront 'a timeless and impersonal world' and are asked to consider 'the permanence of the impermanent frail flower,' the retreat and return of the little wave on the shingle, we watch the gulls, which have unexpectedly invaded the book, circle and rise and fly off to sea. And we know that it will not be long before Topaz, 'poor volatile bird,' will follow.

(1990)

Two ... aright?: from hymn 487 in the Methodist hymnal
A man ... goes: from 'The Buried Life' by Matthew Arnold

Afterword to *Emily's Quest*

I wish I had been old enough to read *Emily's Quest* in 1927 when it was first published; or – failing that – that I had read it in my early teens. Coming to it as an adult, I can see it only as a period piece – a charming period piece, mind you – but a period piece, nonetheless.

I try to imagine what my responses would have been had I read it earlier. Unquestionably, I would have identified with Emily's wish to write. But because I had two older friends who were reporters on the local paper, it would not have occurred to me that it was difficult for a woman to be a writer, and so Montgomery's feminist concerns would have been wasted on me. I would have understood Emily's love of nature, and her idealistic, romantic view of the world. I would have recognized what she meant by 'the flash' and been fascinated by, and probably envious of, her psychic powers. When I came across, 'Aunt Laura, who owned to a Dr. Fell feeling about Mr. Wallace ...' I would undoubtedly have been pleased that I could complete the verse, 'I do not love thee Dr. Fell.' 'Cremona' and 'simoleons' which I now know to mean 'violin' and 'dollars' would have baffled me then. And I would have been, as I am now, bewildered by the origin of 'spleet-new' – a descriptive enough phrase in context, which is seemingly without derivation.

But as I was also reading Hemingway's *A Farewell to Arms* in my early

---

When I came across ... Dr. Fell: 'I do not love thee, Dr. Fell, / The reason why I cannot tell. / But this I know, and know full well, / I do not love thee, Dr. Fell,' by Tom Brown. Emily's Aunt Laura is objecting to the Rev. Mr. Wallace as a possible suitor for Emily.
spleet-new: 'brand-new'; of Scots origin

teens – covertly, perhaps, and not without trauma – I suspect I would have found *Emily's Quest* too young for me; although, had I read it any younger, it would not have addressed my more childish interests, and I would have found it too old. I think L.M. Montgomery, herself, would have understood my reaction for, in a letter to her friend G.B. MacMillan, she complained that '... The public and publisher won't allow me to write of a young girl as she really is. One can write of children as they are ... but when you come to write of the "miss" you have to depict a sweet insipid young thing – really a child grown older – to whom the basic realities of life and reactions to them are quite unknown. *Love* must scarcely be hinted at – yet young girls often have some very vivid love affairs. A girl of *Emily's* type certainly would.'

In *Emily's Quest*, love is more than hinted at. It is the theme of the book. I can imagine a time when young teen-age girls (not of my generation, and certainly not of the current one, in which twelve-year olds, if they read at all, are said to prefer novels about teen-age abortion) would have found the book a romantic story and even a guide to love. And because of the charm of the book, I cannot help but want young readers for it. I wonder if today a still younger group – more precocious than anything I have dreamed of – independent yet starry-eyed, now gobbles it up.

Emily is attractive to men, and her various love affairs (if one can call them that) might well have alerted young readers to the fact that although English provides us with only one word for it, there are many kinds of love. To Aunt Laura's, 'But there's only one way of loving' Emily replies, 'Oh, no, dearest of Victorian aunties ... There are a dozen different ways.' Who would not have been helped by knowing – preferably before the event! – that if you are at the mercy of *eros* you can be 'in love' one minute and 'out of love' the next? – as Emily was with Aylmer Vincent; and that an immense liking for a person – *agape* – such as she felt for Dean Priest, is not the same as *amor* which she felt for Teddy Kent. In addition, Emily's love for her aunts and tenderness for her uncle Jimmy might be described as *caritas*. L.M. Montgomery helps us see that one word cannot serve for four such different emotions.

In a less knowing age, the book might have been informative and engrossing – for what subject is of greater interest? – not only to adolescents, but to us all. Perhaps something in us recognizes that so strong a passion, or so great a fidelity, or such a willingness to serve or care for another must have links with a love that is higher, and beyond naming.

It was in 1920, after completing six Anne books, that L.M. Montgomery confessed she had 'gone completely "stale" on Anne and *must* get a new heroine.' That was the year Emily was born. The same year also saw her copying passages from Olive Schreiner into her Journal. 'There are as many kinds of love as there are flowers: everlastings that never wither; speedwells that wait for the wind to fan them out of life; blood-red mountain lilies that pour their voluptuous sweetness out for one day and lie in the dust at night. There is no flower that has the charm of all ... The speedwell's purity, the everlasting's strength, the mountain-lily's warmth; but who knows whether there is no love that holds all ... friendship, passion, worship?' To which Montgomery adds 'Yes, I think there must be a love which embraces them all – but it is rarer than a blue diamond ...'

Love, clearly, was very much on her mind. And not without reason. In 1911, when she was thirty-six, having failed to find her 'blue diamond' she married Ewan Macdonald, a minister, for whom she felt no grand passion. ('Those whom the gods wish to destroy they make minister's wives,' she wrote to G.B. MacMillan, her confidant over many years.) And in 1920, towards the end of a long list of things she claimed to *like*, we find 'I like good spruce gum. I like my husband. I like people to like me.')

It is not surprising that she damned with faint praise, for hers was a difficult marriage. Today, there would be a clinical term for her husband's melancholia, which took the form of believing himself predestined to hell. Highly strung herself she kept sane by writing. Between *Anne of Green Gables* in 1907, and *Rilla of Ingleside* in 1921 – in addition to a memoir, articles, stories and poems – she published eleven novels. In February, 1922, two years after she conceived the idea, she had finished *Emily of New Moon*. *Emily Climbs* followed two years later, and *Emily's Quest* two years later again.

I find it hard to see these three books separately – the child is so clearly mother to the woman. They might be one long book which begins magically, for L.M. Montgomery has an extraordinary eye for children. But as

---

Olive Schreiner: South African author of *The Story of an African Farm*

the book progresses and we ask more of it, it becomes thinner, offers us less. When we want soul we are given temperament. It is not that Montgomery has no talent for character. The Emily we meet in *Emily's Quest* is the same Emily we met in *New Moon*, different only in that she spells better, is taller, and finds 'the 'love-talk' that had bothered her so much' in writing her early stories, has become easier. She is a charming young woman, still romantic, idealistic, and passionate.

I also find it difficult to separate Emily from Lucy Maud, herself, who reads Marie Bashkirtseff, *The Story of an African Farm*, Jane Austen, Emily Brontë, the poems of Alice Meynell, Charles G.D. Roberts and Marjorie Pickthall. And who, as a true Canadian (Montgomery was born one year after Prince Edward Island entered Confederation), resists the golden lure of the U.S., as Emily does, convinced that she can write just as well, if not better, in Prince Edward Island. In this belief she is encouraged by an increasing number of literary successes; and, when discouraged – as from time to time she inevitably is – she turns for inspiration to lines from 'The Fringed Gentian' written by an unknown author and published in *Godey's Lady's Book*:

> Then whisper, blossom, in thy sleep
> How I may upward climb
> The Alpine Path, so hard, so steep,
> That leads to heights sublime.
> How I may reach that far-off goal
> Of true and honoured fame
> And write upon its shining scroll
> A woman's humble name.

'It is only newspaper rhyme,' she writes of it, 'and yet through all my childhood and girlhood it was more of an inspiration to me than all Milton's starry splendour. It seemed to me then to express all the secret feelings and desires of my being ...' For further proof of her affinity with the verse, she called her 1917 memoir, *The Alpine Path*, and in her introduction

---

Marie Bashkirtseff: Ukrainian-born Russian diarist, painter, and sculptor.
Alice Meynell: British poet

to it she wrote, 'It is indeed a "hard and steep path."' For a woman of her time, I am sure it was.

In the light shed by the two volumes of Journals (1889–1921), which cover her years from age fourteen to forty-six, it becomes startlingly apparent that I am justified in thinking Emily and L.M. Montgomery have much in common. I draw attention to this with some reluctance. As a writer myself, I find irritating the belittling of the creative imagination implicit in the belief that all fiction is autobiographical. Yet in this case, the similarities cannot be overlooked.

Both L.M. Montgomery and her heroine were high-spirited, fun-loving girls, brought up by elderly relatives who had little understanding of the young; both kept journals; both wanted to be writers; and both had to press to acquire higher levels of education. This is only the beginning. The list could go on and on. (Even the name Emily [M L ee] is almost L.M. backwards with a y attached.) If we still have any lingering doubts as to the origins of Emily, we can turn to the author herself: 'People were never right in saying I was Anne, but, *in some respects*, they will be right if they write me down as Emily.'

Having read the Journals, I can only agree. But one glaring factual difference, among many lesser ones, distinguishes the two women. Emily, unlike her author, marries the man she loves. I cannot help wondering if L.M. Montgomery found vicarious pleasure in giving Emily the 'blue diamond' she would have liked for herself. Emily's own words from *Emily Climbs* persuade me that it is, at least, a possibility: 'I read a story tonight. It ended unhappily. I was wretched until I had invented a happy ending for it. I shall always end *my* stories happily. I don't care whether it's "true to life" or not. It's true to life as it *should* be and that's a better truth than the other.'

It may even be a truer truth. And I think L.M. Montgomery knew it.

(2000)

Afterword to *Nights below Station Street*

Families. A book about families. No lengthy saga, taking you through generations, but an account of one family, a small one at that, set in one time period, which, by the legerdemain of David Adams Richards, becomes the story of many families. All families. And timeless. Or such is the way I see the Walshes – Joe and Rita and their two children, Adele and Milly. Completely different from my family, and completely different from yours – for what two families can possibly be the same? Nevertheless ... I wonder. There must be a common denominator that makes them so recognizable.

On the face of it, my parents were markedly unlike Rita and Joe, my younger sibling a temperamental opposite of Milly, and I doubt that anyone who knew me as a child would dream of comparing me with Adele. We resembled each other only in number. But through Richards' portrayal of the Walshes, I know their family inside out. Even more remarkable, I could almost imagine they know mine. An absurd thought? How could fictional characters possibly know people in real life? It is beyond argument, I agree, but at some subliminal level, I suspect they might.

Poverty, drunkenness, and intermittent violence were not problems common to the Walshes and ourselves. Sometimes on New Year's Day friends of my father's seemed to walk a tilting deck, but my exposure to such sights was occasional and without trauma. It bore no relation to the mixture of rage and loyalty towards Joe that over and over again tore teen-age Adele apart. As to poverty – no – my mother did not have to look after the neighbours' children to keep food on the table. And violence? Never.

But there is something about families, the texture of them, that varies little from one to another, however great their differences. It is that knowing of one another washed and unwashed, sick and well, quarrelling, laughing, weeping, sleeping, that seems finally to pass beyond personality, beyond character even, back to the primal matter of which we are all composed.

The fact that I spent some years in New Brunswick and am familiar with the local slang may contribute to my feeling of intimacy with these people. When Richards writes, *jeesless dope, getting the frig out, some foolish* – he is using expressions that were once so common to my ear that I spoke them without hearing them, rather in the way teenagers today use words I find offensive. We especially liked to make *some* into a superlative. 'Some hot!' we would say, meaning that it was a great deal hotter than very hot – the epitome of hotness, in fact. And 'some cold!' which it frequently was in winter. It is no wonder Richards refers to the weather – snow falling, the wintry nights, the smell of the cold. He is long on smells of all kinds – smells one would normally not think about, smells that challenge one's olfactory imagination – chipped paint, iron in autumn evenings, burnt paper and railway ties, a sky that smelled of ash and darkness.

There is no sexual abuse in this book, no explicit adultery, there are no four-letter words, unless one counts Adele's fine samples of adolescent wit in her invention of Russian names: Alexi Snipmyweineroff, Symka Feelmyarseoff and Seaman Rotchercockoff, inspired by the arrival of a Russian ship and the hockey playoffs.

What makes the book so much more than a sordid tale and elevates it to the level of tragedy is Joe. We watch his ongoing torment over his drinking, his desperate morning-after pick-me-ups of shaving lotion and beer, and his rationalizations, at such times, that it was his nature to drink, that he wouldn't be himself if he didn't. Threats of damnation from the priest, Joe's agonies of contrition that result in his attendance at Alcoholics Anonymous, and embarrassing apologies to Adele – 'the one person he loved more than all the others' – these ups and downs, these bouts of violence and shame should have made a loser out of Joe and a hell of the household. And yet, and yet, they did not. For all his inadequacies, Joe had greatness in him. How could a house be a hell if its inhabitants love one another? Not love, perhaps, in any very obvious ways, but love one another nonetheless, for there are, after all, 'seventy times seven ways of loving,' as George Johnston says.

And perhaps because they love one another the reader loves them too. For the fact is, the reader *does* love them – make-the-best-of-it Rita, lively little Milly, feisty Adele, and, most certainly and especially, Joe. Joe – half animal, half angel, as indeed we all are.

There is a theory that people drink for one of two reasons: either to heighten experience or to diminish it. It seems clear that Joe belongs to the second group. Here we see him, this great strong man with an injured back, for which he would neither take the medicine the doctors prescribed nor rest as advised, submitting only reluctantly to a physical examination in hospital: 'He hated the hospital. He hated to look at the other people there – for the simple reason that he felt he was intruding upon them. For instance, when he'd passed by the X-ray room, he happened to see a woman in a bra folding her shirt carefully over a chair. At any other time he might have thought he was fortunate. But at this moment he felt sad. The bra was very clean and white; as if she was attempting to wear the proper things, and do things diligently now that she was here – just like everyone else in the world.' How many of the people one sees daily would evince so fine a sensibility?

With a few brilliant touches Richards evokes adolescent Adele. 'Adele's nerves were bad. She would not sit at the table if Milly ate beside her. She could not eat her food unless she had Kleenex piled all about her plate, to keep off Milly's breath.' Adele, despite her nerves, and desperate to survive in a dysfunctional family, 'walked out and slammed the door, and headed towards the centre of town, perfume on her jeans.' On her jeans – and can one not smell it! The cheap perfume one's friends gave one for Christmas in one's teens.

Richards' style is non-linear and subtle. The reader might well be caught unawares by Adele's pregnancy for there have been no steamy sex scenes to anticipate it, no suggestive remarks. We have only the most fragile clues as evidence of her condition, clues that might easily be false clues or nothing more than indications of 'a phase,' to borrow the term adults use in attempting to explain the seemingly inexplicable behaviour

---

'seventy times seven ways of loving': 'Veterans' (*Endeared by Dark: The Collected Poems* [Porcupine's Quill, 1990], 83)

of the young. Adele stays in her room more than usual, stops seeing her friends, takes to going to church. Poor, valiant little Adele.

Although mainly concerned with the Walshes, the book casts far wider a net. As if in a tumbling barrel, the minor characters play off one another. There is Adele's boy-friend, Ralphie, who at fifteen had liked a girl he always thought of 'the way you think of a bluebird'; the perverse old doctor who complained that nothing was the same anymore, even as he brought evolution to a halt with his enraged declamation that 'everything is the same and always has been and always will be' – a paradox anyone over fifty will understand! And then there are Myhrra and Vye – Myhrra, half in love with Joe, Vye, object of Joe's jealousy – principal actors in the sub-plot whose wedding sets the stage for what can be described only as an epiphanous ending.

'If Vye had taken any other road he would have been safe,' so begins the final chapter which describes Myhrra and Vye driving off on their honeymoon in a blizzard, becoming stuck in the snow and setting out on foot, separately. '... [Myhrra's] wedding veil came off and blew up in the air. Snow fell down her neck. She slapped at the snow with her hands as if to brush everything away.' What a scene for a movie! Or a ballet.

This note of fatalism continues, builds to crescendo. Richards has known all the time that these lives were playing themselves out as if scripted, but only as the book is ending does he allow the inevitability of it to become apparent. 'Yet by not finding the road – and by taking a turn to the left because of a windfall that tore her dress ...'; 'For if she had done anything else, moments sooner or moments later ...'; 'or taken another direction ...'; 'or stopped for any longer ...'; 'or got out of the car any later ...' He makes it clear that the pattern fits together with the intricacy of a jigsaw puzzle.

At the same time Ralphie, a mile under the earth and unaware of his child being born, instead of railing at the events that had made him into a miner and not a lab technician as he had hoped, felt, instead, special. 'An object falls, it has no ideas where it will land, but at every moment of its descent it is exactly where it is supposed to be.'

For his part, as the wedding celebrations ended, Joe started out towards the hospital and Adele, but for some reason he didn't understand, he had turned onto the road to his camp in the woods. 'He had every intention of going up to see his child and grandchild ... and yet at every point on his journey he was doing other things.' In the snowy woods 'Joe felt that everything was here, and everything here was exactly the way it should be.'

And how it 'should be,' for Joe, was that he should pour his bottle of vodka into the snow, tie on his snowshoes, and following unexpected tracks that only an experienced woodsman would be able to read, come upon a lost and exhausted Vye whom he carried on his back toward his truck. 'His back pained only slightly but he did not feel it so much – not knowing the processes of how this had all happened, only understanding that it was now irrevocable because it had.'

Richards sees not only the generosity of the human heart, and the grandeur of the human spirit, but the rarely-glimpsed, and more important still, cosmic design that is stamped upon us. He has deeply understood the apocryphal tale of the old lady who fell down an elevator shaft and, discovered at last, and asked what had gone through her mind as she lay there, had replied that every atom in the universe was in exactly the right place.

(2003)

Darkinbad the Brightdayler: The Work of Pat Martin Bates

Suppose a person of the Fourth Dimension, condescending to visit you, were to say, 'Whenever you open your eyes you see a Plane (which is of Two Dimensions) and you infer a Solid (which is of Three); but in reality you also see (though you do not recognize) a Fourth Dimension, which is not colour nor brightness nor anything of the kind, but a true Dimension, although I cannot point out to you its direction, nor can you possibly measure it.'

Edwin A. Abbott

The circles began in the early sixties. White circles on white – the colour of fresh snow, common salt, swan's plumage, milk or cream; black circles on black – the colour of night, of soot, of coal or tar; silver circles casting a lunar glow; white circles on black, black circles on white – spinning,

---

'"Darkinbad the Brightdayler," on the art of Pat Martin Bates, appeared in *Canadian Art*. It has since been republished (in a slightly altered form) in the catalogue for a recent exhibition of her work at the Art Gallery of Greater Victoria' (PKP).

Darkinbad the Brightdayler: 'Going to dark bed there was a square round Sinbad the Sailor roc's auk's egg in the night of the bed of all the auks of the rocs of Darkinbad the Brightdayler' (James Joyce, *Ulysses* [Random House, 1986], 607).

Pat Martin Bates: a Canadian artist and professor of fine arts at the University of Victoria since 1965. She is known especially for her innovative printmaking. In an unpublished poem, 'For PMB on Seeing Her Glass Room through a Toothache Darkly,' Page describes her experience of attending an exhibit of Bates's work while suffering from a toothache.

'Suppose a person ... measure it.': Edwin A. Abbott, 'Preface,' in *Flatland*, 5th ed. (Barnes & Noble, 1963), xiii

dislimning 'as water is in water'; still. Symbolic of All, of One, of Nothing. Enigmatic, paradoxical. The Whole and the Hole. An enclosure for concentrating energy. The Wheel of the Seasons, the Dial of the Hours. The Cosmic Clock where Past and Future are one.

'Circles are the first thing a child draws,' says Pat Martin Bates, who has taught children. 'The dot is the first universe of God.'

We are in her living room overlooking the Pacific. Gulls trace parabolas in the bright air. Plexiglas cubes – six-sided prints of black and silver circles – in diminishing size like the parts of a Chinese Box, rise in a corner of the room, breaking and reflecting light, altering space.

She eases prints from a black case – prints which seem larger than the area we stand in; and I am reminded of the hypothesis of two contemporary mathematicians, that you can slice an ordinary sphere such as an orange and then reassemble the slices to form spheres smaller than atoms, larger than suns. Looking at her circles I am persuaded of such a possibility. By some conjuring the same circumference increases and grows small.

'What is that atom greater than the Whole?'

Squares, rectangles, triangles, mandorlas, polygons follow – singly or combined – shape within shape. Black for the occult or hidden wisdom, intuition; white for understanding, consciousness; silver, the light of the moon which originates with the sun; black-and-white signifying that light, which is understanding, comes from darkness, as day from night. (While we associate black with death, a less materialistic people knew death as re-birth. The Kaaba, Cubic Temple in Mecca, is draped in black; black the Stone, reputedly cast down from Heaven; and black the original

---

dislimning 'as water is in water': 'The rack dislimns, and makes it indistinct, / As water is in water' (*Antony and Cleopatra* 4.14.10–11). See also 'all matter blurs, unsteady, seen through water / and I, in him, dislimn, water in water' ('Water and Marble,' *HR* 2: 62).

hypothesis of two contemporary mathematicians: a reference to the Banach–Tarski paradox, first stated by Stefan Banach and Alfred Tarski in 1924, that it is possible to take a solid ball in three-dimensional space, cut it up into finitely many pieces, and reassemble the pieces into two balls of the same radius as the original

'What is that atom greater than the Whole?': Compare "Concealed in the heart of all being is the Atman, the Spirit, the Self; smaller than the smallest atom, greater than the vast spheres" ('Katha Upanishad,' part 2, in *The Upanishads*, translated with an introduction by Juan Mascaró [Penguin, 1965], 59).

mandorla: A mandorla is 'an almond-shaped panel or decorative space, usually framing an image of Christ' (*OED*).

banner of the Prophet Muhammad. In Old English, *black* was often confused with *blac* meaning white or shining. And carbon – the element most characteristic of life – crystallized, becomes diamond: durable, everlasting, white octahedron, eight-faced.)

'For me,' says Pat Bates, 'a square is really not an abstract shape. It's more like a window. And a rectangle for me, really is a door, something we could pass through.' Apertures, passages from one world to another. Man's escape hatches.

From the square which is material, terrestrial (the four elements, seasons, points of the compass) through the octagon – an intermediate form – we can travel to the eternal order of the circle. Earth, Air, Heaven: three worlds, the existence of which she is constantly drawing to our attention. By means of ladders (scala – scale) on which we can ascend, or windows and doors through which we can pass, if only in metaphor, we are able to remember for a moment at least, the crucial intersection of this world with eternity. The pictorial equivalent of this overlapping of two worlds is the mandorla – eye-shaped to inform us that here we arrive at a moment of vision, our blindness cured.

Her geometrical figures reverberate in us, reflect deeply hidden images in our minds as in endlessly mirroring mirrors, each reflection adding a new dimension to the simple shape, opening unexpected distances and closenesses as though she had provided us with telescope, microscope, mirror.

As her images have unified and become more compact she has also become increasingly preoccupied with the different densities of matter. She prints on thick papers reminiscent of leathers, their surfaces broken by the coarse grain of the paper and the embossed, often welt-like forms that appear both as image and texture. Initiation cicatrices raised on the skin. In the manner of fifteenth century tinsel prints, she sometimes 'reinforces' or 'thickens' small areas with 'sheen and shine.' Bandages them. I think of the protective bark of trees, the numerous layers of an onion.

No longer content with reflected light, she now pierces the paper – building sharp points into her plate – so that the finished print, placed in a 'Glass Wall,' bridges two lights: source and reflected. Sun and Moon. Matter is losing its opacity.

Additional elements appear. Tiny ink dots, black or white, stipple the already grainy, pitted and pierced surface in small rivulets and traceries, indicating magnetic fields perhaps or bioplasmic matter. And tiny prickings with needles of different sizes to let light through, create areas concave or convex depending upon which side she works from, like a fine rash on the skin of the drawing or the braille characters which provide the blind with 'sight.'

Among her new works are two square diaphanous canvases – (one black, one white) – which shimmer in the air, a veil of darkness, a veil of light. The surfaces, shifting and subtle, dissolve and re-form as a slight change in one's position alters the angle of light shining through their intricate perforations. On the black she has sewn a large black mandorla, like a protective shield. The white has for its centre a small unprotected white heart. I am reminded of a saying of Muhammad, that God hides himself behind seventy thousand curtains – those of light hiding the Divine 'obscurity' and those of darkness veiling the Divine Light.

What is all this sewing, stabbing, piercing, stippling if not tattooing? And what tattooing if not an initiation rite to mark a turning point in the life of tribal man? The principal techniques of tattooing include incision and stitching; of pseudo-tattooing, painting with dot and stipple. But the rituals of transformation are usually accompanied by ordeals. A fully tattooed body, suggests Joseph Campbell, is a 'mythological epiphany.'

Many traditions, myths and ideas converge at this point. One thinks of all the seamstresses and embroiderers through the ages; of the fifteenth century practices of pierced and punched work in printmaking, and from the same period and discipline, of *manière criblée*, which was characterized by a group of dots. (Surprisingly, a seventeenth century definition for the word occult is 'a dotted line.') One thinks of Mexico's Xochipilli, Lord of the Flowers, whose flayed body symbolizes the splitting open of matter to release the seed of new life; and of Xipetotec, Lord of Liberation, always portrayed in a flayed human skin, having freed the initiate from matter and so, from time. The skin then, in Mexican mythology, is a dark rind that traps and hides the being of light within us. One thinks of the rejuvenation rites of Pharaonic Egypt known as 'the passage through the

---

a saying of Muhammad ... Divine Light: cited in Titus Burckchardt, 'The Foundations of Islamic Art,' in *Sacred Art in East and West*, translated by Lord Northbourne (Perennial Books, 1967), 111

'mythological epiphany': *Primitive Mythology* (Viking Press, 1959), 117

manière criblée: a technique of metal cutting using dots to form a design. Page has created several works in a similar technique using a paper punch; for example, *Excalibur's Handle*, *Doily*, and *Four Wings*.

occult: 'of a line, etc.: drawn as an aid in the construction of a figure, but intended to be erased or covered; (also) dotted. Obs.' (*OED*)

skin'; and that the hieroglyphic of three skins knotted together signified 'to be born' – the number, perhaps, referring to man's threefold nature: body, soul and spirit. And finally, closer to home, of the button-decorated ceremonial blankets of the Kwakiutls. As a startling afterthought one realizes that the Golden Fleece was the skin of a winged ram!

For Bates' series of drawings – *Arctic Signal Search in Northern Silence* – one must almost grow new eyes. The subtleties of pale spray upon pale spray, dot, stipple and perforation reveal their secrets only to those patient and still enough to receive them. They suggest vast empty tracts of snow, lighted by a kind of blinding morse; silent – their silences broken by echoing gongs or drums. Who signals? Stars blink in the black and frozen night. Some works in this series are so pale that looking at them it is as if the pupils of your eyes whiten. As if the forms hidden in their blizzards could only be detected through the ear.

Arctic Rose Heads for Above and Below demands your entire attention. This rose is a rose and its mirror image – eight petalled. Above and below the two heads glow, larger, translucent. Together, they form a hexoctahedron – that is, if you were to cut out the two 'roses' and fold them in triangular facets you would make a 48 faceted solid of eight irregular 'planes' composed of six facets. Symbolically the rose is the western equivalent of the lotus, the mystic centre or heart.

This drawing, though still, is mutable. An immensely complex and condensed image. Twin search-lights probing; binoculars two-lensed – like the heart which is two-valved and a double rose – seeking the signal and the signal's source. But the answer lies, as answers often do, in the opposite direction. Hold the drawing up to the glass wall and it breaks into a light so distilled, so diamantine, one feels one has never seen real light before. I suppose there is some law of physics which can explain this intensity. *The Arctic Rose Heads ...*, illuminated from within, bloom in a hoar-frost, sun created. Signaller found.

But Bates' work reveals its deepest meanings when related to the art, architecture and literature of the Middle East. In her working drawings – immense sheets (white or black!) covered with Xeroxed floor plans of Islamic temples, geometrical studies, experimental piercings, careful measurements, quotations, questions to herself ('Do I cook yesterday's

---

eight petalled: About the time this essay was written Page was working on a series of black and white gouaches, displaying eightfold symmetry, *Pieces of Eight*.

potato peelings with today's potatoes?') – you can trace her persistent pursuit of those invisible laws on which all great art must be based. According to Titus Burckhardt, 'Art, to the Muslim, is a 'proof of the Divine existence' only to the extent that it is beautiful without showing the marks of a subjective individualistic inspiration; its beauty must be impersonal like that of the starry sky.'

Pat Bates' concern with the dissolution of matter – symbolic breakthrough to a limitless and immaterial world – a 'spinning place' – is inspired by the intricacies of mosaic and tile, the pierced domes of Muslim mosques and the writings of Jalaludin Rumi, twelfth century Persian poet to whom many of her works are dedicated. The contemplative nature of this artist leads her away from the 'disturbing multitude of things' towards a tensionless equilibrium.

'You know, in a way, I get simpler and simpler all the time,' she says. 'And less personal. This new plate I'm working on is going to be a square. That's all it's going to be – a square ...'

A square – material, earthly. Earthy. A field in which the treasure is buried and which, diligently worked, will yield a golden harvest year after year.

The circling of the square – which for some reason we call squaring the circle – is no less a miracle than turning earth into heaven.

(1971)

Titus Burckhardt ... starry sky.' Titus Burckhardt was a Swiss art historian who wrote on Islamic art and was associated with the perennial philosophy (see note on 'The Perennial Philosophy,' p. 39). The quotation is from Burckhart, 'The Foundations of Islamic Art,' in *Sacred Art in East and West*, 107.
'spinning place': 'So it must have been after the birth of the simple light / In the first, spinning place, the spellbound horses walking warm / Out of the whinnying green stable / On to the fields of praise' (Dylan Thomas, 'Fern Hill'). The concept of 'spinning' occurs frequently in Page's poetry, representing moments of heightened awareness. See, for example, 'Spinning' (*HR* 1: 229).
Jalaludin Rumi: See note on 'Rumi' (p. 68).
'disturbing multitude of things': 'Art clarifies the world; it helps the spirit to detach itself from the disturbing multitude of things so that it may climb again to the Infinite Unity' (Titus Burckhart, 'Introduction,' in *Sacred Art in East and West*, 12)
a field in which treasure is buried: Compare 'It is treasure buried in earth, concealed ... / We saw that it surely was love ...' (Jalaludin Rumi, *Kolliyaat-e Shams-e Tabrizi*, edited by Badiozzaman Forouzanfar, translated by Zara Houshmand [Tehran, Amir Kabir, 1988], no. 1640).

The World of Maxwell Bates

When first I visited Maxwell Bates' studio in Victoria it occurred to me that if some all-powerful ruler decreed artists could inhabit only the worlds they had themselves created, then Bates had equipped himself well. For his world contains landscapes complete with trees, lakes, flowers and rivers; cities with street lamps, shops, houses; houses with furniture, cutlery, plants, toys, pets – even abstract paintings for the walls! And a cavalcade of people: kings, queens, clowns, children, socialites, politicians, poets, lance-corporals, labourers; characters lumpish and asleep as Beckett's Hamm and Clov; hierophants and magicians evocative and mystifying as the figures of the Major Arcanum.

Looking at this flood of work I felt caught by the force of a Gully Jimson. There was a feeling of high tension in the room. A tremendous energy. And as we went through the stacks of water-colours, oils, pen and ink drawings, I realized Bates' world contained too, history and ideas, time and space. Echoes, reminders and comments about painters, writers or politicians were drawn just as freely from ancient Egypt, the Orient, eighteenth century Europe as from contemporary Canada. It was as if he were in fact saying, all time is now: all space is here.

'On coming to Victoria in the late sixties, I once again met up with Maxwell Bates, whom I had known as a child in Calgary. This article was my response to the world his art created. It was published in *Canadian Art*' (PKP).
Maxwell Bates: Canadian architect, painter, and writer
Hamm and Clov: characters in Samuel Beckett's *Endgame*
Major Arcanum: one of twenty-two cards in the tarot deck, depicting arcane symbols
Gully Jimson: artist-hero of the Joyce Carey's novel *A Horse's Mouth*

I had a sense of déjà vu. And not without reason. For this enormous proliferation was a development and natural growth of the work Bates had done as a boy in Calgary: the intricate mediaeval forts, each stone carefully delineated, pennants and flags flying which he had drawn in pencil under an *art nouveau* lampshade in a house with Turkish carpets, bear and ocelot skins on the floor and copies of *The Studio* behind the leaded panes of bookcases.

The beggar-kings, clowns, jokers, ambivalent figures in checks and stripes, wearing medals and badges, cocked hats, tights, chains of office, are descendants of the mosaic panels he made forty odd years ago when camping with my family near Calgary. We used shingles for base, clay from the river bottom for ground, and fragments of coloured glass from a nearby dump. These are his fringe people, citizens of some peripheral world to which Bates, in one of his guises, owns the keys.

In his large oil, *French Town*, a street scene painted in a subtle range of snuff colours, colours of dried vegetation, his two worlds meet. In the background stands a great palpable building – shuttered, chimneyed, occupied. And middle foreground where the eye somehow expects a horse-drawn carriage – a group of men moves towards us – striped, camouflaged, verging on illegibility. Not revellers. Not workmen. Cosmic footballers? They fit no known category. Are they perhaps materializing at this very moment by a trick of light or the angle of one's own gaze? And why the miniature nine-starred constellation at their feet?

Make-up artist, theatrical outfitter, dreamer, watcher. Bates' eyes look out of his face as through chinks in a wall – observant, alive – with an expression of innocent alert objectivity to be seen in the eyes of a wild animal. In his early drawings of Chinese cooks, telephone repairmen – the familiar people of the neighbourhood in which we both grew up – Bates, the watcher, observed physical man – how arms and legs worked, how nose and ears related to eyes and chin. Then the observations extended to man's foibles, absurdities. As social commentator he is immediate, biting. Sometimes almost too wry to be borne. OK, OK, so we are mis-shapen, idiotic, pompous, vile, but are we not sometimes beauti-

---

The Studio: A London art periodical that ran from 1863 until 1963, when its name was changed to *Studio International*.

ful, sometimes ...? And his canvases reply to us, 'No. Not you. Not now. But landscape is beautiful. Look!'

It is as if he is on a train making tart notes on the antics of his fellow passengers while at the same time moving endlessly through changing countryside which he records purely, passionlessly. Winter landscape, summer, spring. The seasons pass on his canvases without indicating in any way how relentless his eye can be as social critic. But to linger on his satire is to miss what I believe to be the larger symbolism.

Anyone who has had a vision of what man could become must thereafter see him in his partial evolution as deformed. 'Man, poor man, half animal, half angel.' Vile only in relation to his possibilities. I believe this to be the essence of Bates' message. ('And in my soul / Feelings of some scarcely perceptible / Great beauty / Some words of God, / Not quite invisible.' Bates' own lines.)

If one is in any doubt, *Scarecrow with Yellow Background* is confirmation. In the figure of the scarecrow we see man. He is dwarfed, immobilized, impotent, made of cast-offs. Abject, frightened. A mockery of everything man should be. Unable to inherit the field of gold which surrounds him. Yet he is aureoled, cruciform. For all his weaknesses and inadequacies, Bates tells us, man is Divine. Details of the painting bear this out. In the brim of the hat we see the symbol for infinity. In its crown half black, half white – the reconciliation of opposites: completion. And the curious checkered patchwork garment the scarecrow wears is surely the motley of the jester – God's Fool.

(1970)

'Man ... half angel.' Page identifies the source of this as 'one of the Middle Eastern poets of the Middle Ages' (e-mail, 15 December 2005).

Max and My Mother

Maxwell Bates must have been about thirteen when our paths first crossed, for I cannot have been more than three or four, and there were ten years between us. I have no memory of him from that time except as part of a larger memory – the house in which he lived, the garden in which he played and the family in which he was the first-born.

Max's father, an architect in Calgary, was 'Uncle Bill' to me, as his mother was 'Auntie May.' In addition, to my brother – yet unborn – they were to be god-parents. (It was 'Auntie May' who called my brother Tommy Bumble after the thumb in the finger family: Tommy Bumble, Mrs. Throstle, Root Whistle, Penny Root and Icky Fee. This absurdity amuses me still!) The Bateses lived in a low-set house on Thirteenth Avenue just off 7th Street next door to the Ranchman's Club, kitty-corner from old Lady Lougheed's stone castle and exactly opposite two rather ugly square apartment blocks. This was my neighbourhood. I knew it well.

Designed by 'Uncle Bill' with special attention – as we always thought – to the Bateses' shortness of stature, the house was beautiful. The rooms may have been of normal height – perhaps it was their proportions that played tricks with my eyes – but certainly, as I sprang up tall in my teens, in their living room I felt like Tenniel's drawing of Alice after she had drunk from the bottle labeled 'Drink Me.'

'"Max and my Mother" appeared in *Border Crossings*. It was a piece of nostalgia' (PKP).
Tommy Bumble ... the finger family: from a poem, 'The Five Finger Folk,' by Olive A. Wadsworth

It is the living room of the house that I remember especially. And it is the living room I see in its various aspects as I look at Max's paintings. A deep-piled carpet of a miraculous peacock blue, bordered with the Greek Key design in black on cream, ran the length of the room. In a small bay, jutting off to the left about half way down the room, and providing space for a writing desk, lay a polar bear skin – almost the same colour as the cream in the rug's border. The bear's glossy head and shining glass eye were delicious to the touch. The furniture – dark oak – was intricately carved, in many cases by the Bateses themselves, and innumerable *objets d'art* – fashioned of silver or ivory – covered the occasional tables: perfect little elephants, photos in silver frames, snuff boxes, patch boxes. It was a long room, the entire end of which was a diamond-paned bow window overlooking, in summer, a stretch of green lawn and a riot of flowers – delphiniums, peonies, phlox, white daisies, and, most magical of all, sweet-smelling mignonette, the flower with the French name. Or, during the long winter, soft and white as marshmallows, the mounded snow.

It was in the bow window that tea was served and my mother and 'Auntie May' and 'Auntie Kit' – Max's real aunt – with their recently shingled heads, cloche hats, short skirts and cigarettes, sat among the cups and saucers – flappers. 'Auntie May' had a face like a white pansy, her dark hair grew in a widow's peak. 'Auntie Kit' her sister, was cheerfully sharp-featured with bright blue eyes. And my mother – how describe my mother? While in one way as invisible to me as I was to myself, in another she was the only one I saw – the centre of my regard. The green light from the garden dappled the three of them, the thin bread and butter, the caraway seed cake, and the two voluptuous white Persian cats that moved to their own slow music.

We children (there were four Bates children, three boys and a girl) although not Max, who was too old, and not Billie, the baby, fingered the keys of the piano at the other end of the room, keys the same colour as the polar bear skin and the rug's border. ('Ramona, when day is done I hear your call.') Or we clustered in the den, where in bookcases behind leaded-glass *art nouveau* doors, lay the latest copies of *The Studio*. And

---

'Ramona ... your call.': from 'Ramona,' a popular song from the twenties, based on a novel by Helen Hunt Jackson about a Native American girl
The Studio: See note on '*The Studio*' (p. 99).

there, around the centre table where Max sometimes joined us under the hanging Tiffany lamp, we supported unwieldy copies of *Chums* and pored over their contents. Or we drew, in our little island of light, above the deep reds and blues of the Turkish carpet.

Was it Maxwell or Newton, his brother, who began all figures with the feet? Newton, probably. Under his pencil, which moved at fantastic speed, pages of comic strip characters sprang upward from their shoes. Max drew forts – stone forts, each stone distinct. When I think of it now, I am surprised forts didn't play a larger role in his later work for – boy and man – they so obviously had significance for him. When I asked, many years later, if it was he or Newton who had drawn forts, his face lit up as he replied, 'Exactly me! Exactly me!' And later still, in the game I have always called 'the Jung game,' when asked to describe his ideal house – unconstrained by geography or bank balance – he described a fort, turreted, self-contained, with its own water and power supplies.

I was often put to bed upstairs in the Bateses' house while my parents played mah-jong in the peacock-blue-carpeted living room. The Bates' mah-jong set was an especially beautiful one and it may have been the painted ivory counters, like silk beneath the fingers which drew them back to the game from time to time. But more often than not, when the four of them were together, they spent their evenings carving quarter-cut oak with matched chisels and wooden mallets. My parents had a practical reason for pressing on with the carving. They were furnishing their house, making stools and chests and cabinets – preferable to the store-bought veneer, about all that was available in Calgary in the twenties, certainly all that was available in their price range. The designs they carved were often *art nouveau*, borrowed from the pages of *The Studio*. Only my mother, claiming she was too stupid to copy – ('all my brain is in my fingers') – drew her own, and attacked her oak with a bravado and flourish none of the others ever matched. They were all good carvers, but her style was different – more impressionistic, freer. She used broader chisels, took broader strokes. When they carved in our much smaller house, I fell asleep to the sound of pounding mallets and ringing laughter – laughter of a kind that would sound somehow old-fashioned, innocent, today –

Chums: a monthly magazine for boys, published between 1892 and 1941. 'These were later bound in the thick, red, hardcover volumes that we read' (PKP).

and I wakened to crisp oak petals littering the floor, sharp and crunchy beneath my bare feet.

The upstairs of the Bateses' house didn't compare with the downstairs. The children's rooms had a barracksy feel about them. I seem to recall iron cots and the racket small boys make with their boots on uncarpeted floors. Max, glimpsed in his room, under a flat light, squeaked away on his newly acquired violin. Only in what would now be called 'the master bedroom' was there some of the wonder of the living room. I remember, especially, the beautiful kimonos that hung casually on the backs of doors – heavy silk kimonos with softly padded hems, and 'coolie coats' made by 'Auntie May' with wide and brilliantly coloured borders of appliqué and embroidery. When I was in my early teens she gave me one as a present and I loved it more, I think, than any piece of clothing I have ever owned. In it, as I studied for my dreaded chemistry exam, I imagined myself an artist, although what kind of an artist, I didn't know.

Her other memorable present to me, when I was much younger – still a child, in fact – was a wired French doll. It was astonishingly sophisticated with its embroidered face, the black and white satins in which it was dressed, and the marzipan cherry tucked into its belt. I loved it – reservedly at first – but as time went on, I grew uneasy with it, frightened even. Each night after I had gone to bed my parents, thinking it would amuse me, placed the doll in a different posture – hanging from a blind, head inside the flour bin, sitting on the kitchen table holding an egg – until I began to think it was alive, and mischievous, if not evil. My final break with it was the day my mother told me I could eat the marzipan cherry. How strange the first taste of almond paste – bitter made to seem sweet, danger so seductively disguised. One bite and I was sure I was poisoned. Where did the concept of poison come from, at that age? Fairy tales, perhaps. But I can still remember my mother anxiously assuring me, reassuring me – that she would never have let me eat it if it were poison. See, she was eating it herself. But I was doubly suspicious of the doll after that and only looked at it sideways.

Our house – 1411 7th St. West, the first address I ever memorized, and the only one I remember now, of all the many places I have lived – was

---

a wired French doll ... sideways: Compare the similarly disconcerting doll episode in 'The First Part' ('That visit finished me for dolls.' [HR, 1: 217]).

one of a row of three bungalows designed by 'Uncle Bill.' It was spacious, one-floored, verandahed, with a full cellar and attic. Later, many years later, it was occupied by Max, who, I understand, used the attic as his studio. When we moved into it in the early twenties, it had been vacant for some time and the cold and the smell of tomcats struck us like sledgehammers. A whole tribe of strays must for some time have made it their headquarters. Nor were they to be easily ousted. The large tom having lost his ears and part of his tail to the frost, was more like a fur bolster than an animal, and unless you caught the flash of fire from his fur-covered eyes, it was hard to tell if he was coming or going. The females were lean as awls. They were used to having the run of the house, and our presence in it, far from driving them out, only improved conditions for them. It was warm, for one thing. Also there was food in the house of which they were quick to take advantage. Even with the basement door shut, they could somehow get into the kitchen. They knew more about the house than we did.

My father finally devised a plan to catch them. Having, thirty years later in Australia, devised a plan to drive a terrified possum out of a house, I know something about such plans. My father's idea was this: at bedtime, he would shut all doors but the one to the basement. To its handle he would attach a rope long enough to reach into my parents' bedroom. He would leave a ham-bone, too large for a cat to pick up, on the kitchen floor and, when they heard the knock of the bone on the floor, my mother would pull on the rope – thus closing the easy escape to the basement – and my father would rush into the kitchen and usher the cat out the back door. So far, so good.

The awaited moment came. Knock, knock. My mother pulled on the rope, my father streaked down the hall to the kitchen and flung the back door wide. The cat, however, with great good sense, made off in the opposite direction, up the hall and through the open door to the bedroom where, my mother insists, it leaped over and under the bed, with my father in hot pursuit. I can imagine my young mother, her heavy chestnut hair looping over her bare shoulders, sitting up in bed, pulling on the rope and screaming with laughter and alarm.

I realize now, that she had been in Canada only three or four years at that time, having married my father who had gone overseas with the first Canadian Division in World War I, and returned to Canada, a war hero, with an English wife, a two-year-old daughter and no job. At the time of the cats I can't have been more than five. Max would have been fifteen.

During the next few years Max gave my mother many of his small sketches: two drawings of Chinese cooks – delicate drawings in coloured pencil; a line-man up a pole – in vigorous pen-and-ink on newsprint; an ink wash drawing of a night scene with fireworks; a May Day parade in which a red flag is the only colour; woodcuts. She greatly admired his work and encouraged him, even to the point of sending a parcel of his drawings to a critic in England – a friend, I think, of her father's, whose name, I believe, was Wellington. He too, was impressed – if Max had never seen Daumier, he was a genius. Of course, he *had* seen Daumier and many years later spoke to me of his influence. But he may have been a genius, all the same.

I have one distinct memory of Max from a slightly later period. My father, being in the army, spent his summers under canvas at the military camp on the Sarcee Reserve, and we with him. One year he undertook to build a wooden shack, finished with tarpaper and shingles – one permanent dwelling to add to our collection of tents. Max, now in his early twenties, was staying with us. Although he later spoke of himself as an acutely shy young man, he was not shy with us. I remember him as short, stocky, sandy-haired, with bright blue eyes and a voice rather like an angry bee.

Under the boundless summer sky, there was nothing to do and everything to do. We could swim in the muddy Bow River – or was it the Elbow? – winding its way icily beneath us at the foot of a steep embankment; we could sing around a bonfire at night; search for puffballs in the prairie grasses, happy in the illusion that the Rockies were within walking distance; explore a nearby dump. Marvellous the objects which can be found if you are not too fastidious. My mother, Max and I collected pieces of coloured glass – gorgeous colours – rich peaty brown, 'eye-glass' blue, deep amber yellow, blood-red, green; and the opaque white or patterned bits of broken pottery. With these as our tesserae, and clay from the riverbed spread on unused shingles as our ground, we made mosaics. Max's, as I remember, were bizarre figures, forerunners of his beggar kings – brightly-coloured, antic, and beautiful – but, because of the nature of the

---

Max ... coloured glass: Compare the account in 'The World of Maxwell Bates' (p. 99).

materials, as impermanent as flowers. We didn't have coloured film, in those days, on which to capture them. And, now, only I remember.

I didn't see Max for some years after that. He worked his way to England on a cattle boat and it was not until I went to England myself when I was seventeen that we met again in London. He introduced me to the Wertheim Gallery, just off Piccadilly, where, as a member of The Twenties Group, he exhibited. And he told me of the painters worth watching for in London, the galleries worth going to. Perhaps he directed me to Stanley Spencer, with whose work I fell so madly in love. Certainly he gave me another window on painting in the London of 1933. And, one day, as we parted in a tube station – he going in one direction, I another – we stopped first at a locker from which he removed some canvases and propped them up against a wall for me to see. Small, brilliantly coloured oils, vibrantly alive in the grey of the underground.

I returned to Canada. War broke out. Max joined the army. Was taken prisoner. Released. Time passed. I saw him briefly when he was on his way back to Calgary again in the forties. I had a small apartment in Ottawa and he came round and had a meal and made some sketches of me. Then I didn't see him again for a much longer period. I heard that he had married, was living in Calgary and working as an architect. That his wife had died. That he had remarried. That he had had a stroke.

It wasn't until the mid-sixties when my husband and I moved to Victoria that I discovered Max, too, was in Victoria. We got in touch with him by phone, went out to visit him in the country where he lived with his wife, Charlotte. He was a travesty of his former self. Locked into an iron support, he moved with what appeared to be excruciating difficulty. It was as if his body was a cage. His square, always determined-looking face, was twisted into a grimace of even fiercer determination. But looking out of it, his eyes seemed more alive than the eyes of anyone I had ever seen. They reminded me of the eyes of a fox I had once stared into at short range – alert and fiercely innocent – taking everything in. Knowing it all.

And he was painting – slashing away with his good arm – great paint-

---

Wertheim Gallery ... Twenties Group: The Wertheim Gallery sponsored the Twenties Group, which was formed to exhibit works by artists in their twenties without charging the usual subscriptions or fees for exhibiting. 'Ecce Homo' (*HR* 1: 17–18) describes Page's experiences in London at this time.

ings, intricate drawings, landscapes, people, patterns, self-portraits. He was, perhaps, in his best period. It was as if by overcoming seemingly insuperable physical difficulties he had been given a new energy. He was like a laser. And Charlotte – gentle and loving – looked after him. But he was restless. Now that he could no longer travel, he must move. No sooner were they settled in one house than he must find another – not just any house but one with adequate storage space and studio. The paintings, the stacks of drawings, had all to find new quarters.

My mother, an old lady now, was in Victoria in a nursing home. Max would occasionally visit her, thumping down the hall to her room with his brace and stick – elderly, seemingly more the age of a brother than the son of a friend. They didn't have a great deal to say to each other – Max was always inclined to monosyllables and Mother said little more than 'Dear Max!' Sometimes I looked on, and as I remembered all the occasions on which I had seen them together, their joint presence conjured up for me the Bateses' living room in Calgary – but seen now as if at the end of a long tunnel – very small, and very brilliant, and about the size of a stamp.

(1988)

Review of *The Company of Strangers*

Nothing prepared me for *The Company of Strangers*. Here, in Victoria, news reports rather than reviews preceded its opening. We were told it was the most popular film at the Vancouver Film Festival. But what does that say? It might even be reason enough to stay away.

I went because I was curious. I had known a Constance Garneau – slightly – in Montreal in the forties and had read two books by Mary Meigs. To the best of my knowledge neither of them acted. There could, of course, be two Constance Garneaus but surely it was beyond probability that there were two Mary Meigs. What kind of a film was this, anyway?

The Roxie Cinegogue where the film was showing is an old quonset hut with some garish drawings in black and red on one of its side walls and two rows of rather seedy-looking loges at the back. It provides us with our only alternate cinema – film festival movies, NFB movies, the *Rocky Horror Picture Show*. Its audience is almost a community: you are bound to see someone you know as you wait for the lights to go down. People wave, swap seats, chat. The noise level is high.

It is perhaps for this reason that the sound is often too loud at the beginning of a show. The night I went to *The Company of Strangers* was no exception. The female voices raised in song in the opening scene were deafening. As were the blasts that announced the demise of the bus and

---

'Film Review of *The Company of Strangers* was written at the request of *Brick Magazine* after seeing what I still regard as a remarkable film' (PKP).
The Company of Strangers: directed by Cynthia Scott (1990)

the screams from the driver who got out to examine her vehicle and tripped and twisted her ankle. I missed some footage immediately after that because I went into the lobby to ask if the projectionist could turn down the sound. Back in my seat I imagined I must have missed the explanation as to why these curiously ill-assorted women were on the bus in the first place. But the second time – for I saw the movie a second time and may well see it a third – although I stayed in my seat from beginning to end I was still none the wiser. Thinking about it since I realize that the open-ended beginning is essential. Essential? Why? I don't quite know why. Perhaps for no other reason than that it balances the beautiful title shot of the group of women materializing mysteriously and slowly out of mist. And yet I think there is another reason. Maybe it will come to me.

We get to know these women as they get to know each other. Constance Garneau, 88, with a cane, walking with Mary Meigs, 71. The bus driver, Michelle Sweeney (a jazz and gospel singer and the only professional actor) limping along on her wounded ankle. The two elderly English women – Cissy Meddings, 76, and Winnie Holden, 77 – and Alice Diabo, 74, a Mohawk from Kahnawake. (I give their names and their ages. Anything less would belittle them.) The third English woman, Beth Webber, 80, and Catherine Roche, 69, a Catholic nun with the Order of the Sacred Heart, are not among the vanguard setting off across the green field to the wonderful house Constance has promised them – Constance so filled with memories of place. We are in Laurentian country, *en plein été*. The white-throated sparrow is singing his high needle-sharp song.

Nothing happens and everything happens. They find the house which is not the house. They share the remains of their picnics – one apple cleverly cut into seven sections by Mary Meigs, some chiclets, half a sandwich, an orange. They take their pills – for arthritis, bladder, angina. Drink water from the lake where, at dusk, the swallows skim its surface for flies. Sister Catherine Roche tinkers with the engine of the bus as she listens to 'Jesu Joy of Man's Desiring' on her Walkman and sings along. (She, by the way, has a Ph.D. in Music Education.) And Beth Webber, young for her 80 years and holding onto her youth with a bright desperation, stays aboard the broken down bus in preference to venturing into the unknown country.

The women improvise beds, settle down. As perfect day follows terrible night, they search for food, create fish traps from panty hose, birdwatch, paint – or Mary Meigs paints. She is marvelously inquiring, humorous, self-contained. The world for her is full of interest. They are short of food, deprived of comforts, forced to come to terms with their circumstances, with each other, themselves.

The wonder of it is they are not acting. They are playing themselves. They are inventive, good natured, adaptable, humorous – Cissy, whose adoring husband, now dead, helped her learn to walk again after a stroke; Winnie who had been a belly dancer in her youth; Alice who worked in a bottling factory; Beth unable to speak of her grief; and the nun, bride of Christ, cut out for sacrifice and joy. They laugh. They tell their stories. They talk of love. Of suffering. Of fear of death. But how can I tell you their conversations? Some things are trivialized if they are retold. They have to be heard the first time. They have to be exchanged. That is it – confidences have to be exchanged.

If I think of the film in one way, I see it as a long green flowing continuity – a kind of banner with birds and music, splendid music. If I think of it in another, it is a series of perfect vignettes that recreate whole lives for us, that remind us of our friends, ourselves. I think of the back view of Constance as she walks alone through the field towards the lake, uncertain of her footing. Of Constance – laughing her girlish delighted laugh – when she bluffs in a poker game. Of Cissy and Alice – their shared grief and their recovery from it. Of Winnie conducting a movement class and the extraordinary snake-like sinuosity of her arms. (According to the release that accompanied the film, Winnie is said to have 'spent much of her free time on set knitting snakes for the rest of the cast. That's right, snakes.') Of the nun and Mary Meigs talking about prayer. Of Beth in one blinding moment, helped by Michelle to remove her mask. And perhaps most moving of all, of Constance and Mary Meigs and the song of the white-throated sparrow.

So this is human existence, we say to ourselves as the credits roll. How wonderful it is. How valiant we are. How beautiful.

'Are men and women really the same?' a child asks in James Reaney's *Colours in the Dark*. For answer, imagine *The Company of Strangers* with a cast of eight men – an 88 year old with a background in radio, an elderly gay, a

---

Colours in the Dark: a play by Canadian poet and playwright James Reaney, performed at the Stratford Festival and at other theatres

widower recovered from a stroke, a Mohawk, a priest, a salesman and two, less easily categorized. What kind of a film would this have made? I get quite lost in the possibilities. Of one thing I am certain. It wouldn't have been remotely like *The Company of Strangers*.

(1991)

Textual Notes

A Writer's Life

Delivered as the Margaret Laurence Memorial Lecture in 1999 in Halifax, at the Writers' Union of Canada annual general meeting. Published 20 February 2005 on the Internet at <http://www.sentex.net/~pql/brazil2.html>

3   Although] It is far from easy for me to address the topic, *A Writer's Life*, for although
3   for me of ... true of] for me with poetry. Less true with
4   excited us and – contrasted] – contrasted
4   which selects] that selects
6   from thoughts] from thoughts or emotions
6   possibly a form] occasionally a form
7   take responsibility] be blamed
8   refuge in the] immediate refuge in my
8   my school friends] that my school friends
8   taken in the fact that] taken in that
8   imagination, certainly no Canadian literature] imagination
10 paper shortage] wartime paper shortage
11 it was as near] it was as close
12 Europe. Naturally ... war effort.] Europe.
13 without something ... publishing] that I didn't contribute to. I published
13 teeth and was entitled] teeth. Entitled,
14 I have never] I had never
15 In 1967 ... McClelland & Stewart] In 1967 McClelland & Stewart

16　more poets;] more poets; poets had multiplied;
16　I would have to] I, too, would have to
16　many things] many other things
16　I actually enjoyed it] but that I actually enjoyed it
16　I would never be put] it would never appear
17　F.R. Scott's] F.R. Scott's *Is*:
18　Joy Coghill] Joy Coghill, and is currently in production as a movie
19　Better still] Or better still
20　Finnish national epic] Norse saga
21　'The beautiful ... concealed from us.'] Beauty is the manifestation of secret laws of nature which, were it not for their being revealed through beauty, would have remained unknown forever.
22　So, where do I go] Where do I go
22　one of the ... ¶I] a most privileged life and I

Safe at Home

Published in *Western Living,* Victoria edition, Winter 1999, 13–17

23　my mother created] my mother drew
23　around a village square] around the village square
24　perfectly to accompany] to perfectly accompany
25　performed ... 'operation,'] the 'operation,' performed on the bravest of us
26　Silver Jubilee of George V] Coronation of George VI
28　which ... picks] which, as he picks
28　as the place] for the place

Falling in Love with Poetry

Published in *New Quarterly* 96 (Fall 2005): 10–12

29　Was it ... soul?] Someone, I think it was AE (George Russell), said that metrics correspond to something in the soul.
29　They certainly ... indeed,] Certainly it is
30　technique: ... rhyme] technique – the slant rhyme
30　Owen; or] Owen. Or

30 rhyme; alliteration] rhyme. Metaphor, alliteration
30 Kay Smith and myself] Kay Smith and me
31 define the word? ... big stretch!] define it? The definition must be broad enough to embrace the many beauties of the world – Aztec art and the art of the ancient Greeks, the Willendorf Venus and the Venus de Milo.
31 'The beautiful] 'Beauty
31 that 'rarely] 'the rarely
31 Here, I suppose ... Vertigo's] ¶recall a story from the *New Testament* Apocrypha – or one very like it. It concerns a child who lives in perfect harmony with his royal parents. His surroundings are beautiful, as are his clothes. There is no flaw in his life until one day his parents tell him the time has come for him to go on a journey to a distant land and there he must find a jewel and return with it. And so he sets forth to a world that is totally unfamiliar to him, where he is strangely unfamiliar to himself, where he remembers nothing of his past life, doesn't even know there is anything to remember. The food of the country is heavy. It puts him to sleep. He is as helpless as if he were bound hand and foot. ¶But his parents are aware of the plight of their son and they write him a letter that reminds him of his mission. And so he renews his quest and retrieves the jewel. Whereupon his clumsy clothing falls from him and he puts on his beautiful robes again. And then he remembers that he is the son of a king. And when he remembers he is drawn back to the world of his fathers – a realm of dazzling beauty that he knows at last for the place where he truly belongs.

Had I Not Been a Writer, What Would I Have Been?

Published in *Brick: A Literary Journal* 50 (Fall 1994): 35–6. The essay is untitled; it is part of a series of essays by various writers under the general heading 'What I'd Be If I Were Not a Writer.'

32 The only use ... parties] High kicks, the splits, sudden controlled falls, and a contorted and impossible climb through a broom to show off at parties were the only uses to which I put that inheritance.
32 nib, to trace the delicacies] nib to the delicacies
32 that way ... Chance] that way. ¶Chance
32 lived ... short supply] was living; nor were there too many art galleries in those days

33 any old part] any old part, although I did
34 world] society
34 *their* mote ... in *my*] their mote through the beam in our

Questions and Images

Published in 1. *Canadian Literature* 41 (Summer, 1969): 17–22 (CL) (2). *The Glass Air: Selected Poems* (Oxford University Press, 1985): 187–91 (GA1); (3). *The Glass Air: Poems Selected and New* (Oxford University Press, 1981), 212–16 (GA2)

40 by earthquake] by the earthquake CL, GA1, GA2
41 Al-Ghazali's angels] Rumi's angels CL, GA1, GA2

Traveller, Conjuror, Journeyman

Published in (1). *Canadian Literature* 46 (Autumn, 1970): 35–40 (CL); (2). *The Glass Air: Selected Poems* (Oxford University Press, 1985), 183–6 (GA1); (3). *The Glass Air: Poems Selected and New* (Oxford University Press, 1981), 208–11 (GA2)

44 'Life Story Briefly Told.'] *Conjectural Biography.* CL, GA1, GA2

Afterword to *A Flask of Sea Water*

Published as 'A Note from the Author,' in *A Flask of Sea Water*, illustrated by Laszlo Gal (Oxford University Press, 1989), n.p.

48 When small] When young
48 read ... parents] parents who read them to me – parents
48 That ... I read] Now that I am older, I approach
48 Even more important] And, even more important
49 fairy story ... Webster] fairy story myself – a traditional fairy story. But I was never able to do so. And then, one night, the phrase 'blue blood' came into my head. Webster
49 family' ... 'Blue] family.' The Shorter Oxford – to quote again – says, 'tr. Sp. *sangre azul* claimed by certain families of Castile as being uncontaminated [sic] by Moorish, Jewish or other admixture; probably founded on the blueness of the veins of people of fair complexion.' ¶'Blue

49 of course!] of course! Why hadn't I seen it before
49 sea – to that] sea – that
49 symbolizes wisdom] represents wisdom
49 truth. And] truth – and as a result, in whose veins flowed, symbolically again, blood that was (sea) blue. ¶And
49 – did it ... have] perhaps, in some Golden Age, 'blue blood' had
49 notion ... Perhaps] notion. Perhaps
50 wisdom ... us?] wisdom – perhaps that happens only in fairy tales.
50 curiously, checking on] interestingly, when checking rulers ... ruled.] rulers, I found that three – Solomon, Alexander the Great, and Charlemagne – had no clear titles to the kingdoms they ruled, and that the fourth – Haroun el-Rashid, Charlemagne's friend – had a curiously unconventional line of ascent.
50 fairy story] fairy tale
50 in which – I might add – the phrase 'blue blood' is never mentioned, but in which] in which
50 makes] made
50 to the sea and returns to the Court with a flask of sea water.] to the sea.

Fairy Tales, Folk Tales: The Language of the Imagination

Based on a talk given in the 1980s at a children's festival in Vancouver and, later, Nanaimo. Previously unpublished.

Foreword to *Hologram*

Published as 'Foreword,' in *Hologram: A Book of Glosas* (Brick Books, 1995), 9–12

The Sense of Angels: Reflections on A.M. Klein

Published as 'The Sense of Angels.' *Jewish Dialog*, Passover, 1973, 18–19

64 older than me] older than I
66 Ibn al-Arabi's] Rumi's
68 unregenerate] unregenerated

Notes on Re-reading George Johnston

Published in (1) *Raddle Moon*, October, 1984, 96–8 (RM); (2) untitled, *Journal of Canadian Poetry* 1 (1986): 50–2 (JCP); (3). *Malahat 78 Review* (1987): 67–72 (MR); (4) *Canadian Notes and Queries* 66 (Fall and Winter 2004): 6–8 (CNQ). RM contains a review of *Taking a Grip: Poems 1972–1978* (The Golden Dog Press, 1978), corresponding to the first part of the essay, up to '"the big summing up."' JCP consist of a review of *Ask Again* (Penumbra Press, 1984), corresponding to the second half of the essay, beginning 'How Johnstonian the title ...' MR contains both reviews, presented separately. The first is entitled 'Notes on Re-reading George Johnston' and is not identified as a review. The second is identified as a review and is untitled. CNQ combines both reviews in a single essay.

69 in which] CNQ; from which RM, MR
71 The Gisli Saga] RM, MR; The Saga of Gisli CNQ
72 not soon was I] not soon I was RM, MR, CNQ
73 up.' ¶***¶ How Johnstonian] up.' How Johnstonian CNQ
73 Marriages, Births, Deaths] Marriages, Births and Deaths JCP, MR, CNQ
73 who knows that] CNQ; who knows JCP, MR
75 so should ... aloud] must be read as such JCP, MR; should be read aloud CNQ
75 'looms' conjure] MR, CNQ; 'looms' – that conjure JCP
75 'doom' and] MR, CNQ; 'doom' – JCP
75 Chorus,' and] MR; Chorus,' JCP; Chorus' and CNQ
76 distance. In] MR, CNQ; distance, in JCP

Afterword to *The Innocent Traveller*

Published as 'Afterword,' in *The Innocent Traveller,* by Ethel Wilson, New Canadian Library (McClelland & Stewart, 1990), 238–43

79 short story] short stories
80 myriad] myriad of
80 – surprisingly ... born] – surprisingly – before she is born
81 first poem ... might] first poem might

Afterword to *Emily's Quest*

Published as 'Afterword,' in *Emily's Quest*, by Lucy Maud Montgomery, New Canadian Library (McClelland & Stewart, 1989), 237–42

84 *Anne of Green Gables* ... 1921] *Anne of Green Gables* in 1908, and *Rilla of Ingleside* in 1920
84 which begins] that begins
84 magically, for] magically –
85 passionate. ¶ I also ..., who] passionate. She
85 And who, as] And as
85 resists the golden] she resists the golden
85 the U.S., as Emily does] the United States
85 Gentian' ... *Book*] Gentian'
85–6 'It is only ... it was.] That L.M. Montgomery was, herself, inspired by the same verse seems evident from the fact that she called her memoir *The Alpen Path*.
86 the two volumes ... Emily] her journals, it is startlingly apparent that Emily
86 turn to the author] turn to L.M. Montgomery

Afterword to *Nights below Station Street*

Published as 'Afterword,' in *Nights below Station Street*, by David Adams Richards, New Canadian Library (McClelland & Stewart, 1988), 227–32

87 so recognizable] recognizable as families
87 father's] father
87 tore] tears
88 hockey playoffs] 1972 hockey series
88 Anonymous, and embarrassing] Anonymous, embarrassing
88 Joe had greatness] Joe has greatness
89 the fact ... love them –] the reader *does* love them:
89 take the medicine ... a physical] rest nor take the medicine his doctors prescribed, reluctantly submitting to an
90 he always thought] he thought
90 to crescendo] to a crescendo
90 all the time] all along

90 hoped, felt, instead] hoped, was feeling, instead
90 For his part ... Joe] Joe, for his part, as the wedding celebrations ended,
90 he had turned] had turned
91 would be able to read] could read
91 the rarely-glimpsed, and more important still,] but even more important, the rarely glimpsed
91 discovered at last,] when discovered

Darkinbad the Brightdayler: The Work of Pat Martin Bates

Published as (1) 'Darkinbad the Brightdayler: Transmutation Symbolism in the Work of Pat Martin Bates,' *artscanada* 28, 2 [nos. 154–5] (April-May 1971): 35–40 (*AC*); (2) in *Pat Martin Bates: Destinations, Navigations Illuminations* (catalogue for exhibition at the Art Gallery of Greater Victoria, 8 April – 10 July 2005 (*PMB*)

93 as day from night] day from night AC, PMB
95 'sight.' ... What] AC. 'sight.' ¶What] PMB
95 The surfaces] AC; Their surfaces
95 tribal man] PMB; primitive man AC
96 Kwakiutls] AC; Kawkiutl AGGV
96 For Bates' series] For Pat Bates' latest AC
96 Arctic ... Below] The most recent of these, *Arctic Rose Heads for Above and Below*, AC
96 translucent] translucent, multi-petalled AC
96 like the heart] as the heart AC
96 But Bates' work ... Middle East.] PMB; It is by relating Bates' work to the art, architecture and literature of the Middle East that it reveals its deepest meanings and one sees the extent to which she has been influenced by that tradition. AC
97 the writings of Jalaludin Rumi] the writing of Jalaludin Rumi AC, PMB

The World of Maxwell Bates

Published as 'Maxwell Bates: The Print Gallery, Victoria, February–March, 1970' *artscanada* 27 (April 1970): 62

98 in the room] about the room
99 bookcases] bookcase doors

99 camping ... We.] he
99 towards us –] towards one,
99 Bates, the watcher,] the watcher
99 worked ... related] work, how nose and ears relate
100 while] and
100 in any doubt] in any doubt about this message
100 mockery of everything] mockery of all
100 opposites: completion] opposites – completion

Max and My Mother

Published in *Border Crossing* 7 (October 1988): 74–6

101 Max and My Mother] Max and My Mother: A Memoir
101 Maxwell Bates] Max
101 Fee. This absurdity amuses me still!) The Bateses] Fee.) They
101 Thirteenth] Eleventh
101 blocks ... well.] blocks.
101 Designed ... house] The Bateses' house, designed by 'Uncle Bill' – designed, as we always thought, with special attention to the Bateses' shortness of stature –
102 especially. And] especially. It was a long room, the entire end of which was a diamond-paned bow window overlooking, in summer, a stretch of green lawn and a perennial border. (Mignonette. The marvellous French sound of its name and the wonder of its smell!) And
102 patch boxes ... winter] patch boxes. And through the end window, a riot of flower colours – delphiniums, peonies, phlox, white daisies. Or, in winter
102 the centre of my regard] my centre
102 clustered ... carpet] clustered around the table in the den where Max sometimes joined us. There, under the hanging Tiffany lamp, we supported unwieldy copies of Chums and pored over their contents. Or we drew, in our little island of light, above the deep reds and blues of the Turkish carpet. Inset on either side of the fireplace were bookcases with leaded glass art nouveau doors, containing the latest copies of The Studio.
103 fingers which] fingers, that
104 after I had gone to bed] before bed

105 he would shut ... he would attach ... my parents' ... He would leave] they would shut ... they would attach ... their ... They would leave
105 the knock ... floor] its knock
105 easy escape] escape
106 daughter] child
106 in vigorous] vigorous
107 film ... on] film in those days on
107 told me of] told me
107 the London of 1933] London of 1933
107 And ... parted] And as we parted
107 going in one direction] taking one tube
107 died ... stroke] died, that he had had a stroke. That he had remarried.
107 Charlotte ... looked] Charlotte, gentle loving, Charlotte looked
108 one house] a house
108 drawings, had] drawings had
108 seemingly more] more

Review of *The Company of Strangers*

Published in *Brick: A Journal of Reviews* 40 (Winter 1991): 38–9

109 Here, in Victoria] In Victoria
109 NFB] National Film Board
110 I don't quite know why] I don't quite know
111 bride of Christ] bride of the church
111 Of suffering] Of grief
111 if they are retold] if retold
111 poker game] game of cards

Index

academe, 16
Acts of Thomas, 27n
Adaskin, Murray, 19
Akhmatova, Anna, 60
al-Arabi, Ibn, 66
Alexander the Great, 50
al-Ghazali, Abu Hamid, 41
Alice in Wonderland, 101
allegory, 53
al-Rashid, Haroun, 50
Anansi, House of, 16
Andersen, Hans Christian, 5, 24
Anderson, Patrick, 11, 12, 63
another order. *See* larger reality
another realm. *See* larger reality
another world. *See* larger reality
Anpu and Bata, 54
anthropology, 33–4
arabesques, 45
Arabian Nights, 5, 54, 64
archetypes, 53, 54, 66
architecture: in Brazil, 35, 65, 66; Islamic, 97; in Mexico, 37–8
Arnold, Matthew, 81
art, functions of, 22

art, varieties of: arabesques, 45; art nouveau, 7, 99, 102, 103; Australian aboriginal, 14; baroque, 14; illuminated manuscripts, 45; Islamic, 31, 96–7; Mexican, 31, 37–8; modern, 10
Art Gallery of Greater Victoria, 92n
Arthur, King, 55
artist, role of, 19
art nouveau, 7, 99, 102, 103
Atwood, Margaret, 16
Auden, W.H., 9, 30, 59
Austen, Jane, 85
Australian aboriginal art, 14
autobiography, xi, xii, 35n, 86

Banach–Tarski paradox, 93n
bark drawings, 14
baroque art, 14
Bashkirtseff, Marie, 85
Bates, Maxwell, xvi, 7, 101–8, 98–100
Bates, Pat Martin, xvi, 92–7
Beach Holme Publishers, 20n
Beckett, Samuel, 98
Benedict, Ruth, 33
Bettelheim, Bruno, 56

Bevington, Stan, 15
Bible, 55
Birney, Earl, 13, 16
Bishop, Elizabeth, 31, 60
bissett, bill, 45, 46n
Blake, William, 26, 29, 59
blue blood, 49–50, 53
Book of Common Prayer, 27
Boots libraries, 8
Border Crossings, 101n
Borges, Jorge Luis, 30
Brazilian architecture, 35, 65, 66
Brewer's *Dictionary of Phrase and Fable*, 49
Brick, 32n
Brick Books, 58n
Britten, Miller, 10
Brontë, Emily, 85
Burckhardt, Titus, 97
Byatt, A.S., 52

Calvino, Italo, 51
Campbell, Joseph, 21, 56, 57, 95
Canada Council, 11, 13, 16
Canadian Art, 92n, 98n
Canadian Broadcasting Corporation, 13, 16, 20
Canadian Forum, 13
Canadian literature. *See* Anansi, House of; Anderson, Patrick; Atwood, Margaret; Beach Holme Publishers; Bevington, Stan; Birney, Earl; bissett, bill; *Brick*; Brick Books; Canada Council; Canadian Broadcasting Corporation; *Canadian Forum*; *Canadian Literature*; *Canadian Notes and Queries*; *Canadian Poetry*; Canadian Writers' Union; Carman, Bliss; Chambers, Jack; Coach House Press; Cohen, Leonard; *Contemporary Verse*; Djwa, Sandra; Dragland, Stan; Eliot, Leslie; Finch, Robert; Grier, Eldon; Haworth, Peter; *Jewish Dialog*; Johnson, Pauline; Johnston, George; Kennedy, Leo; Klein, A.M.; Lampert, Gerald; Lester & Orpen Dennys; MacEwan, Gwendolyn; Macmillan Company of Canada; *Malahat Review*; McClelland, Jack; McClelland & Stewart; Montgomery, Lucy Maud; Mowatt, Don; New Canadian Library; *New Provinces*; *New Quarterly*; *New Statement*; *Nights below Station Street*; Ondaatje, Michael; Pickthall, Marjorie; Pratt, E.J.; Porcupine's Quill; *Prairie Schooner*; Press Porcepic; *Preview*; Purdy, Al; Reaney, James; Richards, David Adam; Roberts, Charles G.D.; Roberts, Goodridge; Rosenblatt, Joe; Ruddick, Bruce; Ryerson Press; Scott, F.R.; Seton, Ernest Thompson; *Six Montreal Poets*; Smith, A.J.M.; Smith, Kay; Sutherland, John; Waddington, Miriam; Wilson, Ethel; Woodcock, George; Writers' Development Trust; Zwicky, Jan
Canadian Literature, 35n
Canadian Notes and Queries, 69n
Canadian Writers' Union, 3n
Canadian Poetry, 13
Carey, Joyce, 98
Carman, Bliss, 30
Carrington, Leonora, 15

Carter, Angela, 52
Chambers, Jack, 45, 46
Charlemagne, 50
Charlie's Aunt, 24
Chekhov, Anton, 33
Chelsea Flower Show, 26
Chums, 103
Cinderella, 54
Coach House Press, 15n
'Cockles and Mussels' (popular song), 24
Coghill, Joy, 18
Cohen, Leonard, 45
Coleridge, Samuel Taylor, 8, 29
communism, 12
Company of Strangers, The (film), xvi–xvii, 109–12
concrete poetry, 45, 67
Contemporary Verse, 13
Coomaraswamy, A.K., 57
court metre, 71–2, 74–5
Cox, Marian Roalfe, 54–5
cummings, e.e., 45, 61

Dali, Salvador, 21
Daumier, Honoré, 106
de Campo, Augusto, 67
de Campo, Haraldo, 67
Debussy, Claude, 4
Deichmann, Erica, 10
Dickens, Charles, 33
Dickinson, Emily, 30
Djwa, Sandra, 16
Donne, John, 30, 59
Dostoevsky, Fyodor, 12
Dragland, Stan, 21
Dr. Dolittle, 24

dreams, 11, 18–19, 38–9, 39n, 41, 56
Drummond, William Henry, 8, 30

egg tempera, 15
Egyptian mythology, 95–6
Eliot, Leslie, 29n
Eliot, T.S., xi, 9, 12, 30, 59
Emerald Tablet, The, 38n
Emerson, Ralph Waldo, 21n
Emily's Quest, 82–6
Endgame, 98n
eternal order. *See* larger reality

fairy tales, 5, 19, 20–1, 48, 51–7, 64
families, 87–8
Faust (opera), 24
feminism, 52
Finch, Robert, 30
Finnish mythology, 20
Flatland, 92
folklore, 5
folk tales. *See* fairy tales
Freud, Sigmund, 56, 64
Fuller, Thomas, 31

Gauguin, Paul, 33
George V: Silver Jubilee, 26
Gisli Saga, The, 71
global warming, 18
glosa, 21, 58
Goethe, Johann Wolfgang von, 21, 31
Gogol, Nikolai, 12
gold leaf, 15
Gorky, Maxim, 56
Graves, Robert, 21
Greek mythology, 53, 96
Grey, Zane, 9

Grier, Eldon, 17
Grimm, Jacob and Wilhelm, 5, 51

Hamm and Clov (characters in *Endgame*), 98
Happy Families (card game), 23n
Hari-Hara, 39
Haworth, Peter, 13
Hemingway, Ernest, 82–3
hemispheres of the brain, 6, 29, 56–7
Herbert, George, 45
Hesse, Hermann, 44–5
higher realm. *See* larger reality
Hoffenstein, Samuel, 30
Homer, 55
Hopkins, Gerard Manley, 30, 59, 61
'Hound of Heaven, The,' 39n
Hughes, Ted, 31
Huxley, Aldous, 39

Ibsen, Henrik, 10
illuminated manuscripts, 45
images, xiv, 35–42, 57, 94
imagination, 10–11, 51–7
Innocent Traveller, The, 77–81
Irwin, William Arthur (Page's husband), 3, 20
Islamic architecture, 97
Islamic art, 31, 96–7

'Jewel Song, The.' *See Faust*
Jewish Dialog, 62n
Jiménez, Juan Ramón, 61
Jimson, Gully (*The Horse's Mouth*), 98
John of the Cross, Saint, 39
Johnson, Pauline, 8, 30
Johnston, George, xiii, xv, xvi, 89, 69–76

Jung, Carl, 11, 39, 41, 56, 103
Just So Stories, 24

Kaaba, 93–4
Kalavela, 20
Keats, John, 8
Kennedy, Leo, 30
King, William Lyon Mackenzie, 26
Klee, Paul, 43n, 45, 46n
Klein, A.M., xiii, xiv, xv, xvi, 12, 30, 62–8
Kwakiutl mythology, 95–6

Lampert, Gerald, 17
larger reality, xiv, 5, 18, 22, 28, 36, 38, 40–1, 53, 64–5, 68, 94, 97
Lawrence, D.H., 38
Le Guin, Ursula, 52
Lessing, Doris, 56, 66
Lester & Orpen Dennys, 15
Lévi-Strauss, Claude, 55
Lewis, C.S., 39
Longo Editore, 21n
Lönnrot, Elias, 20n
Lorca, Federico García, 30, 59, 61
love, 83
Lowry, Malcolm, 38
Lurie, Alison, 52

Mabinogion, 54
MacEwen, Gwendolyn, 61
Macmillan Company of Canada, 10, 13, 77–8
magazines. *See Border Crossings; Brick; Canadian Forum; Canadian Literature; Canadian Notes and Queries; Canadian Poetry; Chums; Contemporary Verse; Jewish Dialog; Malahat Review; New Quar-*

terly, New Statement; Poetry (Chicago); *Prairie Schooner, Preview; Raddle Moon; Studio, The*
magic, 45
Maid of the Mountains, The (musical comedy), 24
Major Arcanum, 98
Malahat Review, 69n
mandorla, 94, 95
Marina, Duchess of Kent, 26
Marvell, Andrew, 59
Marx, Karl, 11, 64
masks, 39, 41
McClelland, Jack, 13
McClelland & Stewart, 13, 15, 16
McGlashan, Alan, 41
memory, 4, 43–4, 64, 66, 94
metaphor and religion, 68
metre, 21, 29
Mexican art and architecture, 37–8
Mexican mythology, 37–8, 95
Meynell, Alice, 85
Mitchell, Stephen, 60
modern art, 10
Monet, Claude, 45
Montgomery, Lucy Maud, xiii, xvi, 82–6
Moore, Marianne, 60
Morgan, Charles, 8
Mowatt, Don, 13, 20
Muhammad, 94, 95
music, 24
myths: Egyptian, 95–6; Finnish, 20; Greek, 53, 96; Kwakiutl, 95–6; Mexican, 37–8, 95

National Film Board of Canada, 13

nature and the environment, 4, 7, 14, 18, 19, 35–7
New Canadian Library, 77n
New Provinces (1936), 30
New Quarterly, 29n
New Statement, 13
New Testament Apocrypha, 27
Nights below Station Street, xvi, 87–91
Nijinsky, Vaslav, 32
nursery rhymes, 64

om, 28
Ondaatje, Michael, 16, 20
Origen, 40n
Ornstein, Robert, 56–7
Osiris, 39
other worlds. *See* larger reality
Owen, Wilfred, 30
Oxford University Press, 16, 20n, 48n

Page, Lionel F. (father), 87, 24–5
Page, Michael Henry Elvy (brother), 24, 87
Page, P.K.
  acting, 10, 33
  art shows: Art Gallery of Greater Victoria, Victoria (1965), 40; Galeria de Arte Mexicano, Mexico City (1962), 39; Picture Loan Society, Toronto (1960), 39
  brother, (Michael Henry Elvy Page), 24, 87
  creative process: fiction, 48; poetry, xi, 3, 6, 46–7, 48, 61; visual arts, 46–7
  culture shock, 40
  doll, 104

father (Lionel F. Page), 24–5, 87
Governor-General's Award for
  Poetry (1954), 14
husband (William Arthur Irwin), 3,
  20
images, xiv
mother (Rose Laura Page), 23–5, 87,
  101–8
painting media: egg tempera, 15;
  gold leaf, 15
places lived: Calgary (1919–24), 23–
  4, 101–7; Winnipeg (1924–7), 23,
  24–5; Calgary (1928–34), 4–8, 30,
  32–3, 99, 106–7; England (1934–5),
  8–10, 25–6, 107; New Brunswick
  (1936–41), 10, 26, 87–8; Montreal
  (1941–4), 11–13, 26, 60, 63–4, 66–7;
  Victoria (1944–6), 98; Ottawa
  (1946–53), 107; Australia (1953–6),
  13–14, 105; Brazil (1957–9), 14–15,
  26, 33–7, 62–3, 67; Mexico (1960–
  4), 6–7, 15, 37–40; Victoria (1964–
  2006), 15–21, 40–2, 107–8
poetry readings, 16
relationship between poetry and
  visual art, 14–15, 36, 40, 43–7,
  67

Page's works
  anthology: *To Say the Least: Canadian
    Poets from A–Z* (1979), 16
  children's literature: *Flask of Sea
    Water, A* (1989), 20, 53–4, 48–50;
    Goat That Flew, The (1993), 20, 54;
    plays for children, 10; *Travelling
    Musicians, The* (1991), 19
  fiction: *Sun and the Moon, The* (1944),
    10, 13; *Sun and the Moon and Other
    Fictions, The* (1973), 10n, 13, 16;
    'Unless the Eye Catch Fire,' 18
  film script: *Teeth Are to Keep*, 13
  non-fiction: *Brazilian Journal* (1987),
    15, 20, 60; Mexican journal
    (unpublished), 15; 'Questions and
    Images,' 15–16; 'Traveller, Conju-
    ror, Journeyman,' 15n
  poetry: 'Address at Simon Fraser
    University,' 19; 'Ah, by the
    Golden Lilies,' 36n, 61n; 'Airport
    Arrival,' 46n; 'Another Space,'
    18–19, 39n; 'Bark Drawing,' 14n;
    'Crow's Nest,' 71n; 'Current
    Events,' 8n; 'Desiring Only,' 12;
    'Ecce Homo,' 9n; 'Filled Pen,
    The,' 31, 47n; 'First Part, The,' 7,
    104n; 'Fly: on Webs,' 36n; 'For
    PMB on Seeing Her Glass Room
    through a Toothache Darkly,'
    92n; 'George Johnston Reading,'
    71n; 'Gold Sun, The,' 59–60;
    'Hologram,' 58–9; 'I, Sphinx,' 20;
    'Kaleidoscope,' 46n, 60; 'Little
    Reality A,' 61n; 'Morning,' 46n;
    'Moth, The,' 8n, 10; 'No Flowers,'
    12n; 'On Being Ill,' 8n; 'Poor Bird,'
    22, 60; 'Prediction without Crys-
    tal,' 11n; 'Shipbuilding Office,'
    11n; 'Skyline,' 46n; 'Spinning,'
    97n; 'Stenographers, The,' 11n;
    'Stories of Snow,' 42; 'Truce,' 17;
    'Typists,' 11n; untitled poem on
    Napoleon (earliest poem), 9–10;
    'Waiting to Be Dreamed,' 5, 38n;
    'Water and Marble,' 93n
  poetry collections: *As Ten as Twenty*

(1946), 13; *Cry Ararat!: Poems: New and Selected* (1967), 15; *Evening Dance of the Grey Flies* (1981), 18; *Glass Air: Selected Poems, The* (1985), 19; *Glass Air: Poems: Selected and New, The* (1991), 19; *Hidden Room, The* (1998), 21; *Hologram* (1994), 21, 58–61; *Metal and the Flower, The* (1954), 13; *Poems: Selected and New* (1974), 16; *Rosa dei vente* (Italian translation of 'Compass Rose') (1998), 21

visual art: *Doily*, 95n; drawings included in *Cry Ararat! Poems: New and Selected* (1967), 15; drawings included in *The Glass Air* (1985; 1991), 19; *Excalibur's Handle*, 95n; *Four Wings*, 95n; *Garden, The*, 19; *Pieces of Eight*, 96n

Page, Rose Laura (mother), xvi, 23–5, 87, 101–8
Parker, Dorothy, 30
Pavlova, Anna, 32
perennial philosophy, xviii
Perrault, Charles, 5
Peter Pan, 24
Piano, The (film), 52
Picasso, Pablo, 21
Pickthall, Marjorie, 8, 30, 85
Pignatari, Décio, 67
poetry; concrete, 45, 67; court metre, 71–2; metaphor and religion, 68; metre, 21, 29; nursery rhymes, 64; prosody, 10; readings, 16; and sound, 46, 75; sung, 45; technique, 30, 71, 75; written, 45
Poetry (Chicago), 13

Porcupine's Quill, 21n
Pound, Ezra, 9, 12
Prairie Schooner, 22n
Pratt, E.J., 30
Pre-Raphaelites, 4
Press Porcepic, 16n
presses. See Anansi, House of; Beach Holme Publishers; Brick Books; Coach House Press; Lester & Orpen Dennys; Longo Editore; Macmillan Company of Canada; McClelland & Stewart; Oxford University Press; Porcupine's Quill; Press Porcepic; Ryerson Press
Preview, 11–13, 63, 64
primitive, the, 41
prosody, 10
Purdy, Al, 16

Raddle Moon, 69n
Raine, Kathleen, 31
'Ramona' (popular song), 102
Reaney, James, 111
Richards, David Adam, 87–91
Rilke, Rainer Maria, 30, 39, 59, 60, 66, 68
Rimbaud, Arthur, 9
Roberts, Goodridge, 12
Roberts, Charles G.D., 30, 85
Rosenblatt, Joe, 62n
Rossetti, Dante Gabriel, 4
Ruddick, Bruce, 12, 63
Rumi, Jalal al-Din Muhammad, 68, 97
Rushdie, Salman, 52
Russell, George (AE), 29
Russian ballet, 9, 10
Ryerson Press, 13, 16

Sanai, Hakim, of Ghazna, 46
scalds, 71–2, 74–5
Schreiner, Olive, 84
Scott, Cynthia, 109n
Scott, F.R., 11, 12, 17, 30, 63, 64
Seferis, Giorgos, 58
Seton, Ernest Thompson, 8
Shah, Idries, 42n, 55, 57
Shakespeare, William, 16, 29, 55, 93n
Shapiro, Karl, 34
Shaw, George Bernard, 10, 12, 33, 63
'She Is Far from the Land' (song), 24
Sibelius, Jean, 20
Simon Fraser University, 16
Sitwell, Edith, 9
Six Montreal Poets (recording), 63
Smith, A.J.M., 12, 30
Smith, Jori, 12
Smith, Kay, 10, 30
socialism, 12
Solomon, 50
Spender, Stephen, 61
spinning place. *See* larger reality
St. Vincent Millay, Edna, 30
Staines, David, 77n
Stevens, Wallace, 30, 59–60
Stratton-Porter, Gene, 8
Studio, The, 99, 102, 103
subjectivity, tyranny of, 41–2
Sufism, 41n, 47n, 55n, 66n, 68n
surrealism, 5, 15
Sutherland, John, 13
symbols, 37–8
synaesthesia, 9

tarot deck, 98n
Tate Gallery, 26
tatooing, 95
teaching story, 51n, 57
Tenniel, John, 101
Tennyson, Alfred Lord, 16, 29
theatre, 24
Thief of Baghdad, The (film), 53
thirty-six just men (Jewish tradition), 66
Thomas, Dylan, 30, 45, 46n, 97
Tobey, Mark, 36, 45, 67
Tolstoy, Leo, 12, 33
'Trees' (poem), 4
Twenties Group, 107
'Two are better far than one' (poem), 81

ultimate reality. *See* larger reality
Ulysses, 92n
Upanishads, The, 93n
Upward Anguish, The, 6n

Valente, Francesca, 21
van der Post, Laurens, 55
Van Gogh, Vincent, 33
Venus de Milo, 31
Vierek, Peter, 34

Waddington, Miriam, 67
Walpole, Hugh, 8
Warner, Marina, 52
Webster's Dictionary, 49
Willendorf Venus, 31
Wilson, Ethel, 77–81
Woodcock, George, xiii, 15, 20, 35n
Woolf, Virginia, 8–9
Word behind the word, the. *See* larger reality

Wordsworth, William, 16
Writers' Development Trust, 3n

Yeats, William Butler, 9, 12, 30, 49, 59

Zen, 39
Zwicky, Jan, 58n